THE BIGFOOT PHENOMENON

Josh Turner

FIRST EDITION

Cover Design: Sybilla Irwin

Illustrations: Alec Julias

Cover & interior layout: SMAK Graphics, Inc.

Editing: Beth Wojiski

ISBN: 979-8-218-24542-9

PARANORMAL
ROUND TABLE

Acknowledgements

I would like to thank the many people who have made this book possible. My biggest and greatest thank you goes to God and my Lord Jesus Christ, my savior, for all that I am, all that I have, and my salvation. Special thanks to Barton Nunnelly, an incredibly talented artist and writer, who I am truly blessed to have in my life. Barton helped me interview the people whose stories are presented in this book and compile the data, which was invaluable to me. I absolutely treasure his friendship. Barton is the author of one of the best cryptid books I have read called *The Inhumanoids: Real Encounters with Beings that Can't Exist*, which will captivate you from beginning to end.

A very big thank you to the editor, Beth A. Wojiski, for all the hard work she contributed. I am forever grateful for her participation in all of this. I know her job is not easy and for that, I thank you. I would like to acknowledge Ms. Sybilla Irwin as well. I appreciate the artwork that you have created, especially for the cover of this book. You have imprinted in my heart forever with your exceptional friendship and your everlasting artwork. Thank you.

I'd also like to acknowledge all the people who provided the encounters that are presented in this book. I am honored to share with the world all you have shared with me. Be proud of yourselves because it takes a brave person to share such encounters publicly. I'd like to take this opportunity to thank the many, *many* listeners of my podcast, *Paranormal Round Table*. Without the Paratroopers and their never-failing support and immeasurable loyalty, I would not have written this book. Thank you.

I want to recognize and give gratitude to Ken Gerhard, Lyle Blackburn, David Weatherly, and Nick Redfern for your inspiration and long-standing friendships. Thank you. I would also like to thank my godson, Alec Julias, who did the artwork for this book.

Thank you to my brothers for always having my back. Your loyalty and brotherhood are unmatched and absolutely irreplaceable.

Josh Turner, 2023

THE BIGFOOT PHENOMENON

THE BIGFOOT PHENOMENON

Foreword by Nick Redfern

Bigfoot: it's a controversy-filled word that is instantly recognizable to just about one and all. And, regardless of whether one is a true believer, an open-minded skeptic, a definitive non-believer, or a semi-interested observer of the controversy, pretty much everyone knows what the word implies and describes: a large, hair-covered, ape-style animal that is said to roam, and lurk within, the mysterious, forested wilds of the United States.

The number of people who claim to have seen a Bigfoot is, now, in the thousands. The beast has been the subject of big-bucks, hit movies. Today's world of reality television loves the legendary monster – viewing figures make that abundantly clear. It occupies the minds and weekends of monster hunters and creature seekers everywhere, each and every one of them hoping to be the person who finally bags a Bigfoot and, as a result, goes down in history.

But, there's more to Bigfoot than that. In fact, there's far more.

The term, "Bigfoot," was created in 1958, when huge, apelike footprints were found in Del Norte County, California. We have a journalist named Andrew Genzoli, of the *Humboldt Times*, to thank for coming up with the famous, monstrous moniker. It's a fact, however, that giant, lumbering, hair-covered, upright creatures have been encountered in the United States for centuries, and long before "the B word" was even a dim blip on anyone's radar.

Ancient Native American lore tells of the legendary, and sometimes savage, beasts that were as feared as they were revered. Encounters with violent, so-called "wild men," of thick woods and ice cold, frozen mountains, were regularly reported in the pages of 19th Century-era American newspapers.

Photographs and film-footage – of varying degrees of credibility and clarity – purport to show the elusive animals, in action, so to speak. Audio-recordings exist of the creatures' eerie chatter and bone-chilling screaming. Startling witness accounts abound. There are whispers that elements of the U.S. Government have the bodies of several Bigfoot on ice, hidden at some Area 51-style, secret installation. There are claims of a UFO link to Bigfoot. Theorists suggest the reason why we lack a body of a Bigfoot, and the reason for their near-mystifying, overwhelming elusiveness, is because the creatures are the denizens of a vast underworld; animals that spend most of their time living in dark caves and deep caverns, unknown to man, and which extend and spread out for miles underground.

Then, there is the matter of the *other* Bigfoot-like creatures. That's right: while Bigfoot – also known as Sasquatch - is certainly America's most famous unknown ape, it's far from being a solitary monster. Florida is home to the Skunk Ape. Southern Arkansas has the Beast of Boggy Creek. Texas is the domain of the Lake Worth Monster. In fact, the creature has been seen in every single U.S. state – aside, reportedly, from Hawaii, which is not surprising, given that it is not connected to the mainland.

Bigfoot, and somewhat similar creatures, extends widely, and wildly, outside of the United States, too. Australia can boast of its own equivalent to Bigfoot. Its name is the Yowie. And, just like Bigfoot, the Yowie is a towering, hairy, man-like animal, one best avoided at all costs. In China there are reports of a similar creature, the Yeren. The Abominable Snowman – also known as the Yeti – forages on, and around, the vast Himalayas of Tibet. The cold, harsh landscape of Russia is the territory of the Almasty. Even the people of England and Scotland claim to have such legendary beasts in their midst. The names of the animals of the U.K. include the Big Grey

Man, the Beast of Bolam, and the Man-Monkey.

Moving on, and demonstrating that there are very few places on the planet that do not appear to be home to cryptid apes and monkeys of very strange kinds, there is the Orang-pendek of Sumatra, India's Mandeburung, the Kikomba of the Congo, Pakistan's Bar-manu, the Hibagon of Japan, Cuba's Guije, and the Mumulou of the Solomon Islands. And that's just barely touching upon what amounts to a vast, monstrous menagerie of Bigfoot-like creatures seen across pretty much the entirety of the globe.

With all that said, it's now time for you to join me on a strange, wild, and sometimes terrifying, journey into Bigfoot's A to Z world. It's a world dominated by the man-monster in reality, in history, in folklore, in movies and entertainment, in the domain of conspiracy theorizing, in the world of the supernatural, and, quite possibly, in the wild, dark woods of just about here, there, and everywhere...

Preface

....

IS BIGFOOT REAL?

People ask if I believe in Bigfoot. The answer is yes! And how could I not, when my own wife swears that she saw one as a young child back in the early eighties? She was just four years old but remembers it well.

"It was early morning," she begins. "The sun was out and shining. Me and my brother, who was three years older than me, and my sister, who was a year and a half younger than me, were playing inside by the window. I had my back to the window. I was talking to my brother, who suddenly stopped answering me, so I looked up at him to see what he was doing because he was sitting directly in front of me. That's when I realized he's got this look on his face like he's terrified. I thought it was just another one of his tricks to make me look behind myself so he could scare me. I called his name again, louder. Then I realized he wasn't looking at me. He was looking past me at the window. So, I turned, and I looked, and I saw what he was looking at. It was a hairy creature with long white hair all over it looking in the window. It had big blue eyes and was human-shaped—but it wasn't human. Up to that point, I didn't know that these things weren't supposed to exist. I just thought it was some kind of monkey man because, around that time, my mom had gotten me a subscription to *National Geographic* or some such that sent out cards with different animals on them, so I just thought it was an animal that I hadn't read about yet.

"So I stood up and went to the window, and I remember telling my younger sister to 'Look. Look!' And she said, no, that she was too scared. So she just stayed with her back to the window and her eyes closed, and my brother stayed there frozen in place just staring at it. I went to the window, and I thought, 'Oh, it's a monkey!' But it wasn't a monkey. It had the shoulders and arms of a person all covered in white hair. It stepped closer, and I put my hand up on the window and it put his hand on the window, too, where my hand was. I don't know why I did that. I just remember the thought came into my mind, and I didn't want to do it, but I was compelled to, so I just put my hand on the window. I turned around to my brother and said, 'Look! It's friendly.' And my brother just started shaking his head and saying, 'No, no, no . . .' So I turned back around and asked if it was hungry.

It seemed to smile at me, and I turned around and started for the front door to let it in so I could make it a sandwich. Then my brother grabbed me and told me he would break my neck if I let that thing in the house. I kind of laughed a little at that, but then I looked into his eyes and saw how scared he truly was, so I said, 'Okay. I won't let it in the house.' So, I turned and walked back to the window where it was standing, and I just stood there staring at it. Eventually, I turned and walked away from it and left it there. I don't remember much after that, but my brother and I did talk about it quite often for days afterwards."

Folks, I've traveled to six continents, and everywhere I've gone it's always been the same: People see the strangest things. Ghosts, UFOs, flying men, black-eyed kids . . . and monsters. Dogmen, Goatmen, Mothmen, Lizardmen . . . and Ape-men. All across the earth, from every continent, sincere people from all walks of life—from poor mountain folk to rich and famous celebrities, from construction workers to scientists—all have soberly attested to witnessing creatures or entities whose existences have been denied or well-hidden by the powers that be who officially spin the continual false narratives about our world and the creatures that live both upon and underneath its surface. These narratives have guided us, as a society and as a species, in the wrong direction for the last two hundred years.

It is, in fact, true that creatures such as these do exist. What they are, on the other hand, is still anyone's guess, but in the last few decades there have been some incredibly intrepid and intelligent individuals who have taken a hard look at mysteries such as these—and they've made some extremely intriguing guesses when it comes to these so-called cryptids. One such person, a Kentuckian named Barton Nunnelly (whose book, *The Inhumanoids: Real Encounters with Beings that Can't Exist,* along with my own terrifying experience with one of these things when I was fifteen years old, inspired me to pursue more extensive research into the phenomenon), strongly disagrees with the use of the term to describe creatures such as Bigfoot and Dogman, claiming that it is a woefully inaccurate descriptor of the entities in question.

Cryptids are natural animals which are rumored to exist, but have yet to be scientifically classified, like the coelacanth, okapi, and giant squid," he told me during one of our first conversations a couple of years ago. "This is clearly not what we're dealing with here. These things are not animals, but quasi-human, with some apparently supernatural tendencies and abilities thrown in which go far beyond anything that modern science has the capacity, as yet, to adequately explain."

I've met Barton and, as an experiencer myself, I completely agree with his position. *Inhumanoids* is a much better term for these human-animal chimeras.

The most well-known Inhumanoid in history, by far, is the creature called Bigfoot, or Sasquatch. There must be hardly anyone left on the planet who hasn't at least heard these terms and know what they represent, although most of them may laugh at even the slightest possibility of these giant, hair-covered creatures' existence. The average person with no interest in the subject might assume, just as the most ardent detractors and skeptics of the reality of Bigfoot claim, that the phenomenon can't be real; that it is a relatively new one, only springing into existence in the late 1960s when two extremely lucky "good ole boys" named Roger Patterson and Bob Gimlin were able to film "Patty" as she walked across a sand bar in a creek bed in the remote forests of Bluff Creek, California, but the "hairy, cannibal giant" is actually a cultural archetype as old as mankind.

Yes, I did say "cannibals," because that's what they were known to be in ancient times. Twenty-five hundred years ago, for example, the ancient Persians believed in the *Al*, a shaggy-haired, swamp-dwelling monster with long tusks and glowing eyes that feasted on human children. The ancient Celts had their evil wood spirits as well, called the *Dus*. Even older still was the infamous beast known as Grendel, whom Beowulf fought and slew. This epic poem is considered the earliest European epic and the highest achievement of Old English literature, and it is most telling to find here a written account of a giant, hair-covered, cave-dwelling Inhumanoid monster that feasted on humans.

Many ancient legends from various other cultures also describe these beings as monstrous cannibals. Everyone has undoubtedly heard of the Abominable Snowman and the *Yeti* from Tibetan folklore, while the Chinese call these things the *Yeren*. Regardless of where in the world you happened to be, seeing these creatures was never considered a good thing. The *Kapre,* for instance, was a frightful entity from the Philippines believed to be big, black, and hairy. It lurked in the darkened forests near pathways waiting to attack and devour unsuspecting travelers. Legend claims that this brutish man-beast was able to put some kind of spell on its unfortunate victims, rendering them helpless to escape its clutches. The Japanese have the *Raju,* hairy cannibal giants with long claws that are particularly active during thunderstorms. Hindu lore tells of the *Rakshasas,* similar cannibalistic beasts with sharp fangs and blazing eyes said to lurk near old cemeteries— something many modern-day monsters still do if eyewitness testimony is to be believed. In Australia, they are known by a variety of names including the *Yowie, Jimbra, Doolaga, Yahoo,* and *Joogabina,* to name but a few. In Bangladesh, locals speak of a hairy, ape-like creature called the *Ban-Manush.*

Of course, Native American peoples also had their legends of these creatures and called them by many names depending on the tribe in question. There were the cannibal demons of the Zuni people, called the *Atahsais*, for instance. Other appellations of the same creatures include *Almas, Almasty, Bukwas, Oh-Mah, Skookum, Yeaho* and *Yakake*, to name but a paltry few examples.

American eyewitnesses, from early settlers right down to modern times, have their own varying regional names for Bigfoot. Missouri has Momo and Arkansas, the Fouke Monster. Arizonians call it the Mogollon Monster. Skunk Ape. Skookum. Grassman and Wood Booger. Ape-man, American Ape, The Big Ones, Bush Indians, Crying Beast, Forest Devil, Hill Monkeys, Wildmen, and Wooly Boogers. The list goes on and on almost to infinity. One could fill an entire book in itself with just the many regional monikers given to these "cryptids." Hundreds and hundreds of different names from as many different cultures worldwide— all describing the same creatures, a fact that all the skeptics and cynics inexplicably deem unworthy of consideration.

Although some say differently, most of these cultures considered Bigfoot to be spiritual or supernatural beings and not animals at all, also a fact that the vast majority of Bigfoot researchers, even those who believe in or have seen these things, all too willingly ignore as if it were the hot potato of the Bigfoot field. Thousands of books, magazine articles, television programs and YouTube videos have been and are still being produced that are dedicated to the complete omission of the reported spiritual aspects and abilities of these beings. Instead, these so-called researchers and investigators of the subject tirelessly and repeatedly offer what amounts to little more than the "I saw Bigfoot cross the road in the headlights of my car" variety of encounters, with no real knowledge of the mystery at hand.

I'm not one of those researchers, and this is not one of those books.

Unbiased research demands that all the details given by an eyewitness must be included in one's investigations before arriving at any sort of conclusion, and that's what I will be doing with this work: taking a hard look at several of the more unusual cases of respected and reliable eyewitness reports—reports that most of my contemporaries would refuse to even consider simply because the data contained within them does not fit their preconceived notions as to the true origins of this species, or even the possibility of the reported events themselves. These are people I've interviewed personally and found to be solid and credible, with previously unprinted and extraordinary accounts of events that do not fit into the stagnant narrative that has been tirelessly spoon-fed to the public at large for the last five decades. People with actual knowledge regarding this enigmatic subject: former law enforcement officials, politicians, scientists, famous actors, and everyday, down-to-earth people. These and more have contributed to this work and are represented here, as well as a few grounded researchers and investigators who diligently seek nothing but the truth, despite the narrative, and follow the facts where they lead—not where they wish them to lead, but they record the data honestly in an unbiased manner and humbly offer it to the public in an attempt to actually take a step forward toward knowledge and understanding of creatures such as Bigfoot.

The presence of these beings in the folklore and myths of nearly every culture in the history of the world, combined with the thousands of reliable, sincere, sober eyewitness accounts right up to the present day, should be enough to convince even the most hardened skeptics of the fact that Bigfoot is, indeed, real! In a court of law, eyewitness testimony has been enough to send thousands of people to death row but, strangely, when it comes to entities of this nature, it is considered anecdotal—or worthless. I find that more than a bit ironic.

I've collected hundreds of firsthand stories from Bigfoot eyewitnesses over the last decade and put thousands of hours and tens of thousands of dollars into research and interviews. One thing soon became apparent when I began this journey of trying to understand the unexplained: authors such as John Keel, Jacques Vallée, and Barton Nunnelly were all right on target when they wrote of the all too apparent connections between seemingly unrelated unknown phenomena—a connection with which nearly all the popular online Bigfoot databases were entirely unconcerned, I also learned. For example, many Bigfoot witnesses, on careful questioning, revealed to me they had experienced other strange phenomena as well, such as seeing unexplainable lights and UAPs (Unexplained Aerial Phenomena) in the same areas in which they saw the creature or creatures. Some had also encountered other unidentifiable animals at some point in their lives. Others had seen out-of-place (OOP) animals or orbs on occasion or had even lived in haunted houses at the time of their sightings. Statistically speaking, the presence of multiple unexplained phenomena should be impossible, yet, like the pioneers before me, I kept hearing it over and over again. Of course, in all fairness, most Bigfoot encounters related to me appeared to be "normal," if that term even applies here, with no paranormal or supernatural elements involved. But more and more, I began hearing accounts that simply did not fit the more mundane, *Gigantopithecus blacki* (or relic hominids) theory, accounts that decried the (as they like to call themselves) apers' theories from the mountaintops to all that will listen, and there's not many, unfortunately.

I've picked as many as time and space would allow for this book, and I hope that, by the final page, you will have at least some of the answers that you're looking for regarding these creatures. In my first book, *Werewolves and the Dogman Phenomenon*, I basically presented many of the stories of werewolves and Dogmen encounters just as I had received them from the eyewitnesses. In this work, what these witnesses have to say is so important to the understanding of this phenomenon, so powerful in its message, that I've chosen to let the eyewitnesses themselves testify on their own behalf, so to speak, and tell their experiences in their own words, and not mine. Hold on to your seat, and let's begin!

1

What Would Jesus Do? – Jesus' Story

Jesus Payan, Jr. is a popular actor who played the hulking, three-hundred-pound bad guy behemoth called "Gonzo" in several seasons of the hit TV shows *Breaking Bad* and *Better Call Saul*. Many fans of those shows might be surprised to know that the actor is a long time UFO eyewitness and researcher. They might even be somewhat shocked to learn that he is also a Bigfoot experiencer. I was introduced to Jesus by a mutual friend and interviewed him for my podcast, *Paranormal Round Table*, in 2022.

One night in 2003, Jesus and a friend of his were out sky watching down a dark, gravel road a short distance from his home in Tularosa, New Mexico, when they heard something walking toward them in the darkness ahead. It was quite heavy, judging by the sound of the crunching gravel, and it sounded like it was walking on two legs. Whatever it was, he said, got to within twenty

19

feet of the two men, then started pacing back and forth at that distance, going faster and faster.

"I got a feeling something bad was about to happen," he told me. "That whatever this thing was, it was working up enough courage to do something to us."

Not knowing what else to do, the two reached down and picked up some rocks and began throwing them in the direction of the sounds, hoping to scare the unseen creature away or at the very least keep it at bay. After the barrage of gravel produced no favorable results, Jesus picked up another rock, closed his eyes, concentrated on the sound of crunching footsteps—and let it fly. This time it was a success! There was no celebration, however, when the rock hit its target and the creature let out an ungodly scream that struck the two men with fear. At that moment, Jesus and his friend took off running for their lives back down the road toward his house.

Halfway there, in the lights of the house and the street, he looked to his left and saw a large, hair-covered creature running down on all fours alongside the road.

Making it back to the trailer at last, the two men beat a hasty retreat up onto the deck and began fumbling with the back door, while the hairy "thing" slammed into the side of the deck. It then ran around to the other side and struck it as well. "It was just a simple sliding glass door," Jesus said, "but at that moment we were so scared, it seemed like I was trying to solve a Rubik's Cube." The two men finally managed to fall inside the back door and lock it behind them. Luckily for them, the hirsute creature decided to exit the scene as well at that point.

Jesus began his acting career soon afterward but returned to the Bailey Canyon area in 2012 to settle down and continue his research—with some success. One night, Jesus went camping in the valley with a friend who had told him he wanted to see Bigfoot. Just after dark, Jesus started to call out to the Bigfoot creatures, saying, "Hey Bigfoot! We're here! Come see us! Come see us!" This caused his friend to become nervous, he recalled. Maybe he didn't want to see Bigfoot after all, out there alone in the woods at night, neither of them armed. But it was too late. The tent was set, the campfire blazing. Nothing to do now but settle in and wait. And wait they did. For several hours nothing happened, and the two resigned themselves to the tent for the remainder of the evening. Just as they were settling down in their sleeping bags, however, the sound of heavy footsteps started to come from outside. Jesus's friend got up and unzipped the tent flap to look out and see what was making the noise. As he was unzipping the tent, a large, hairy arm shot through the opening and knocked him back down. Evidently, Jesus's summons had worked, much to his friend's dismay.

The two then spent a completely sleepless night

inside the tent, during which two different Bigfoot creatures both peeked inside the tent flap to get a better look at its contents while Jesus snapped pictures with his cell phone. At the first break of dawn, they were up and out of there. When I asked him to describe the faces that looked inside the tent, Jesus said, "They both looked different. One had a small, pointed nose with a human-shaped head. The other one had a bigger, more normal nose, a slender face and more hair on the face." It would seem that more than one type of Bigfoot, each with different and distinct facial features, was involved in the event. But that's not all. Jesus claimed that he also captured the image of a third figure on his phone. And it looked just like an alien Gray.

As strange as all of this sounded to me at first, the more that I questioned Jesus, the more the now familiar pattern began to emerge. When asked about his past, he revealed that both he and his entire family had a long history of brushes with unexplained phenomena, starting with a lengthy stay in a haunted house when he was a child.

"My Dad was in the Air Force," he told me. "He was stationed in England for seven years when I was little. We lived in a two-hundred-year-old haunted house. Lots of scary things happened there. Strange noises, knocks on the doors, doors would open and close by themselves. That kind of stuff. My sister's room was always so cold. Nothing we could do would warm her room up, so she usually slept in my room with me. We would hear footsteps on the steps outside our rooms, and no one was on them when we looked. The television would often turn itself on and then change channels all by itself! That's when I first started seeing UFOs." And his involvement with the UFO phenomenon would never really end.

His family moved to the States when he was eight years old, settling in New Mexico in, as luck would have it, another haunted house. As you might expect, events only escalated from this point onward. Spectral figures were seen numerous times there by various members of the household while they also underwent a wide range of poltergeist activity. Jesus told me that once, while he and a sibling were waiting for their parents to get home, it sounded like the TV had turned itself on and started changing the channels on its own, but when they looked, it was still turned off. It was the first time that Jesus began to fear the bizarre entities that had chosen to make themselves known to him. They had a big kitchen table, he told me, with a tablecloth that reached all the way down to the floor. It was under this table that the children sought refuge whenever things would get too scary while they were alone in the house. All the while they were under the table, they could hear what sounded like people playing poker on the table and walking around the kitchen and living room conversing as if there were an otherworldly party going on. This happened several times, he said, and the funny thing was, they could hear all the people talking, but they could never understand what they were saying, as if they were speaking another language. Of course, they never could gather up enough courage to look out from beneath the tablecloth. And who can blame them? During this same time period, strange lights flitted through the skies above their house, both day and night, regularly.

In 1999, when Jesus was twenty-three years old and living in Tucson, Arizona, the UFO activity escalated to an alarming degree, and it was here, he believes, that he was first abducted by aliens. They'd had problems with faces looking in the windows and even rapping on them for attention. Payan described the faces as the "classic alien Grays." They had big, rounded heads and almond-shaped, black eyes with small, rounded chins. Worse still, the entities now seemed perfectly capable of appearing inside the house as well as out. They would hear them running up and down the hallway at night when everyone was trying to sleep or approach a door from the other side and turn the knob. They would knock on the walls of the trailer and even pull the sheets down on a bed where one of the four residents slept. One night, Payan witnessed one of the diminutive aliens standing in the corner of his room watching him from a recess in the wall where an old dresser used to sit. In an effort to get some sleep, they had hung a curtain up in front of the nook. This proved to be for nothing as, from that point on, the entities would now simply pull the curtain aside to continue their observance of the subjects as they slept.

The family soon fled the residence and moved to Las Cruces but, once again, the high strangeness that had crept into Payan's life as a young child would follow him. Once again, the inside of his home seemed to be a popular gathering place for the alien Grays. Jesus had had an alarming dream one night while living there, he told me. He dreamt that an ugly old hag, a witch, was in the room with him mumbling to herself as she levitated him up and off his bed. He weighed over three hundred pounds at the time, and it struck him as odd that the witch could somehow render him weightless. Up he went until his face touched the ceiling of his bedroom. Then, the old crone dropped him. The next morning one of his four roommates asked him, "What in the hell was that loud crash that came from your room last night?" When they examined Jesus's bed, which comprised a box spring resting on the floor and a mattress, they found the box springs crushed, as if a great weight had fallen on them. Jesus also revealed that his mother had experienced these bedroom invaders as well, and she described them to him as having yellowish-gray skin and large, black eyes.

Again, much UFO activity was observed at this location on different occasions by numerous witnesses. So much so that Jesus became known as the "UFO Guy." One day several of the neighborhood kids excitedly knocked on his door and, when he answered it, they begged him to come out, saying there was a UFO hovering in the air above his house.

"I thought they were pulling my leg, at first," Payan recalled. "Then, I finally went outside and saw several people standing on the street, looking and pointing above my house. So I turned around and looked and, sure enough, there was a glowing white disk in the sky directly above my house."

According to Jesus, the disk shot away like a streak toward the Guadalupe Mountains, breaking into three separate spinning disks as it went—all observed by a yard full of witnesses. Strangely, after dark that night, the sky outside was lit up every few seconds by a flash of light like a strobe light. On another occasion, Jesus and another roommate were awakened by what sounded like pebbles being thrown against their trailer. The sounds continued, growing louder and causing much alarm among the men. They rushed outside to find no one there. While they we were standing outside, they heard loud running and stomping noises coming from inside the trailer, Jesus added. "It was really intense and scared us so bad that we went and locked ourselves in the car." Three days later, while at a friend's house, he saw a newspaper that claimed that the recent spate of UFO activity was simply caused by the same old, tired, worn-out explanation that they usually rolled out for public consumption at that time: Weather balloons.

Payan's uncle was working as a dispatcher for 911 Emergency and confirmed that numerous sightings had been called in from the El Paso and New Mexico areas.

Jesus also recalled another strange dream that he felt involved alien abduction, this time while he was living in Texas. He dreamed he was somewhere being examined by multiple types of entities including one type that stood twenty feet tall and resembled the famous Moai statues of Easter Island. These creatures imposed upon him a variety of physical examinations and exercises, to which they seemed surprised that a man of his weight could successfully complete. When he woke up, he was surprised to learn that he had been missing for three days. No one could find Jesus no matter how hard they looked, so they reported his disappearance to the local police.

As it turned out, Jesus's sister ended up working for the police department, and his mother took a job for the US Forestry Service, and both of them were surprised to learn that both departments upheld a similar view when it comes to the Bigfoot phenomenon, at least: They are not allowed to respond to calls where the witness claims to see a Bigfoot. They would respond if someone reported that a person was trespassing on their property, but if the witness claimed to see a big, hairy monster prowling about, the call would be dismissed. I've heard this aspect of the standard operating procedure when it comes to these hairy creatures described many times before. This is usually followed by attempts to intimidate the witness into silence, although it would seem that Jesus has not experienced this aspect of the intricate game that's being played upon the people who encounter Bigfoot and / or UFOs (or both). He has since started a YouTube Channel, *Breaking Bigfoot*, where he shares all these and many other experiences along with all his photographic evidence.

Here we have our first example of the apparent interconnectedness of multiple seemingly unrelated phenomena. Payan feels strongly that Bigfoot are natural creatures with as yet unknown connections to all the other unexplained phenomena that he's experienced. I think it's safe to say that, overall, we don't *know* what these creatures are. But if we listen closely enough with an open mind to the many credible witnesses who have experienced atypical interactions with these creatures, we can get start to get some enlightening clues as to their true nature, their purpose here, and whether they are malevolent or benign toward human beings.

2

A Killer Experience – Rob's Story

June 15th, 2018 was a beautiful, sunny day on Lake Cadillac, Wexford County, Michigan. Rob Karnafel and his girlfriend, Cindy, had rented a cottage and were vacationing there, enjoying the picturesque view of the water and the peace and quiet that can only be found in the great outdoors. On this day, they had decided to rent a small boat and try their luck at a little fishing. They trolled around the lake for a while and, after a couple of hours with no luck at all, Rob decided to abandon the spot and struck out for a new location before giving up for the day.

They went through a canal that led over to Lake Mitchell, then traveled southwest on Lake Mitchell for a while until they found a nice little cove, then dropped anchor. We were ninety feet from the shoreline, he told me, which was straight up and down. There was no beach or anything. The woods came right up to the edge and then it dropped straight down off into the water.

They were there only a few minutes when Cindy told Rob that she believed someone was throwing rocks at the boat. Bewildered, he scanned the tree line carefully but could see nothing. When she complained about it again a few seconds later, he told her, "Honey, there's no one there." Soon afterward, Rob himself saw something falling, apparently, from the sky. He looked up and saw that it was a baseball-sized rock that hit the water with a loud splash. He looked over to tell his girlfriend that she was right, that something was throwing rocks at them, but he never got to utter those words. The first thing he noticed when he looked at Cindy was that her gaze was fixated on the bank. She sat motionless, staring intently in that direction. The second thing he noticed was that Cindy, who was previously sporting a very nice tan, had gone completely pale.

"Her skin was white," Rob said. "She had a beautiful tan before, and now she was white as a sheet. I followed her gaze to the shoreline, and there, standing among the trees at the edge of the forest was this—creature."

He described the creature as being nine feet tall, weighing around eight hundred pounds and covered in reddish-brown hair from head to toe. The front of the chest area was a gray color and the skin on its face, which was almost hairless, was also an ashen gray. It had a human-looking face but, strangely, it looked like a person with Down's syndrome. "You know, they have that specific look. That's what this thing looked like in the face. A human with Down's syndrome."

The thing stood there on two legs with its arms hanging down to its sides, then it raised its arms up and outward, parallel with the shoreline, and began to open its mouth. And then, something terrible happened.

"It was like straight out of a horror movie," Rob explained. "The creature opened its mouth so wide. I mean, the thing's jaw looked almost like it detached from its head and dropped down six or eight inches. The mouth expanded. That's the only way I can describe it. It expanded until it stretched from ear to ear. I looked into this thing's gaping mouth and saw its teeth. It had sharp incisors. Not fangs, but a little longer and sharper than the other teeth. About that time, this thing swung back its arms and roared/screeched/yelled all at the same time without moving its mouth. It was so loud. It sounded like a sonic boom. I don't know how else to say it. We could actually see the soundwave as it came toward us, vibrating the surface of the water before it hit the boat."

At the same time, Rob said, the creature's face drastically contorted into something straight out of a nightmare, going from a Down's syndrome-looking human face to a hideously evil, demonic one in just a couple of seconds—a completely different face that was horrible to look at.

When the sonic blast, or boom, or whatever you want to call it, hit the boat, Cindy, his girlfriend, fell into the water. He tried to turn to his right to help her, but he couldn't move a muscle. He was completely paralyzed. At that point all the colors in his vision seemed to dull. The bright greens of the forest, the blue of the sky and water, the reddish-brown color of the creature's hair, all seemed to fade almost completely to black and white. "It seemed like I was looking through a filter," he told me, "and every second that I stood there, looking at this horrific creature and not being able to move, seemed

like an eternity."

After a few seconds, he shook his head and snapped out of it, then ran to the back of the boat to help Cindy. As he was hauling her back in, he looked back to the spot onshore where the thing had been standing, but it was no longer there. "This was the scariest part, to me, if you can imagine," Rob said. "I'm frantically looking around. I don't know where the thing is. Did it leave? Is it in the water and was coming at us from underwater to attack us? My mind was numb with fear, and Cindy didn't say a word when she was finally in the boat other than, 'Let's get the hell out of here.' I started the boat, throttled the engine up as fast as it could go, and made a beeline back up through the canal and out of Lake Mitchell. We ran wide open until we were back to where we put in. After we docked, I reached over to help Cindy off the boat, and her skin was cold as an ice cube. I probably was too, but I don't remember. We were both in shock, I guess."

And why wouldn't they be? The couple made their way into town, then found a nearby bar, hoping to unwind. Cindy sat down across the booth from Rob. Then the waitress walked up and asked, "What'll it be?"

Cindy didn't drink, Rob stated, but she ordered a shot of Jack Daniels and a beer, which surprised him. "I told the barmaid to bring me the same thing, only make mine a double. When she gets back with the drinks,

Cindy kills the shot of whiskey like a pro. She doesn't even grimace. Then she opens her beer. As I was doing the same, she asked me, 'Robby, what was that thing?' I said that I was about to ask her the same question. Keep in mind that we never talked about anything like this before—UFOs, Bigfoot, ghosts—nothing of the sort. And I told her I didn't know, and she said, 'Robbie, I think it was one of those Bigfoot things.' And I said, 'I think it was, too.' She asked if I thought that we should call the DNR or something. I told her that I did not think that was a good idea, so we went back to the cottage and packed all our stuff and went home. We cut the vacation short because of what happened to us."

As soon as they got home, they started researching the subject, reading about it on the internet and watching YouTube videos trying to figure out what it was that they saw. The closest they could come to was Bigfoot, even though they could not find another example, encounter, or sighting of exactly the type of creature they encountered, one capable of unhinging its lower jaw and transforming its face into an evil, demon-like monstrosity.

Two months later, on August 18th, 2018, Cindy died. "It's not the encounter itself that got me into all this Bigfoot stuff, but the fact that our encounter killed my girlfriend," Rob told me. "I truly believe that. As much as I hate telling this story, I need to tell this story both for me and the people out there. People need to know these things are real and what they're capable of doing. That's why I tell the story. I blamed this creature for Cindy's passing. I wanted to go back to Cadillac Lake with a bazooka or grenade or rocket launcher or something and kill this thing. For Cindy. She was 5 foot tall, 109 pounds. I'm two hundred pounds, and the sound this thing made shook me to my core. I could feel it in my chest, it was so loud. I didn't fall off the boat, but it shook me. I've often wondered if that jarring sound did not do something to hurt Cindy's insides. The doctor said it was a heart attack, but you know, the first time I ever seen her drink was after that sighting, and she did not smoke or do drugs of any kind. She was a healthy woman, so I still to this day, I wonder."

Whenever Rob tells this story, most people blame infrasound for the ill effects that are suffered by some human beings when encountering a Bigfoot. Infrasound is defined as sound waves with frequencies that are below the lower limits of human hearing. In my opinion, this is simply a way of explaining the unexplainable by attributing the infrasound capabilities of normal animals such as tigers and elephants and whales, to a completely unknown and unnatural Inhumanoid entity that doesn't seem at all interested in playing by the rules of nature. Unlike ultrasound, with frequencies greater than 20 kilohertz, infrasound has never been proven to cause measurable harm in humans.

"People say, 'No wait, infrasound can't kill

someone.' Well, I don't really know what this is, but you've got something that's eight hundred pounds standing on the shoreline screaming at you. The depths of this creature's roar, scream, growl—was unimaginable. I mean, it caused a wake that floated toward the boat across the surface of the water. That is some power."

The experience changed him for the worse, and he found himself sinking down into a dark depression after Cindy's death, unable to cope with or rationalize what had happened to them. He had owned a bar in his hometown and had run it successfully for thirteen years, but all that changed as well. "Right after the experience, I called my manager and told him that I wasn't coming in to work. That I was in a very bad spot. I told him to take the money and put it in the bank and not to rip me off. 'I trust you. You'll hear from me when I call you.' And I did not talk to this man again or see him for six months. I didn't even look at my bank account to see if he was making deposits because I didn't really care. I was in full-blown PTSD mode. I was wondering if I went crazy. Then I started having these thoughts that I should never have taken Cindy to the lake that day. That if I hadn't, she would still be alive. That it was all my fault. That I killed her. I went through a lot of things that I don't want to even express to the public."

Things got so bad for Rob that he decided to seek professional counseling. "I went and saw a psychiatrist," Rob confided. "And I've never told anyone that before.

Maybe I was too proud. But today, I'm proud that I did that, and I want to express that to people. That you're not going crazy and there are channels where you can just find someone to talk to about it. I told the counselor that I'd seen a monster. And it took about six months to straighten me out, but I finally got everything turned around, got my business running again. Thankfully my manager was honest and didn't rip me off, as far as I know, and things started getting back to normal again. Well, as normal as they can be after going through something like that. It changed me forever."

Rob claims that the experience has opened his eyes to many things in the past that he dismissed as nothing—until that day. He's sure now that he saw Bigfoot at a young age and, of course, then there are the ghosts. When I asked if he'd ever had anything else unexplainable happen to him, I have to say that I wasn't surprised by his answers.

Oh, yes, he told me. He's seen ghosts and had spectral encounters in his home.

As it turns out, Rob has been seeing ghosts since he was seven years old. "I would see them in my bedroom just standing there, but they were like, you know, something from a cartoon with a kid wearing a sheet over his head, with cut-out holes for eyes. That's what I would see as a youngster, but then I got married when I was twenty-six years old, and I saw the same things again. And I was like, 'What the hell?' I didn't tell anyone and tried not to make too much out of it. So then my brother bought a house, and I spent the night over there the first time about twenty years ago."

Rob's niece, Lauren, was seven years old at the time, and she had always been particularly fond of her uncle. After dinner that night, they retired to their bedrooms. As Rob was lying there in the pitch-black darkness, going to sleep in his brother's brand-new house, the door to his room opened, and he saw the shadowy figure of a little girl standing there in the doorway. He assumed it was his niece standing there, but when he addressed her, she simply backed away, closed the door, and said nothing. Rob thought this a bit strange, of course, but thought little of it. Lauren was just a child, after all, and seven years old was a tender age. However, when the same exact thing happened on his next overnight visit about a month later, he started to become concerned and asked Lauren the next day if she had opened the door to his bedroom the previous night. She said that she had not. Perplexed, Rob assumed that she was simply pulling a childish prank on him, and he mentally vowed that he would be ready if she did it again.

And it did happen again. "The very next time I spent the night there," Rob said, "I was laying there in bed ready when the door opened. It was the same little girl, about four feet tall with long hair. It looked just like my niece. So I said, 'Hey, Lauren, would you like Uncle

Rob to tell you a bedtime story?' Again, she didn't say anything, just backs out and shuts the door behind her. I was prepared this time. I bolt up out of bed and it takes me all of about three seconds to reach the door and jerk it back open. But there's no one there in the hallway. It's empty."

Lauren's room was about twelve feet down the hallway, which wasn't that far. So he raced down the hall to her bedroom door and opened it, and there was his niece snuggled up in her bed sound asleep. "There's no way that she could have run down the hallway, jumped in her bed, tucked herself in at seven years old and be completely asleep," Rob said. "That was what was so strange. I know that now it was a ghost. Thanksgiving rolls around. We were sitting around the table, and I happened to tell my brother- and sister-in-law these stories about my niece. They all looked at each other and they're like, Rob, we see ghosts in here all the time that look like Lauren. And my mom said, in fact, this happened to her too! And then Karen, my sister, told me that in Lauren's playroom, they always looked at the French doors in there. They were glass, and they would see Lauren in the room staring into the closet, talking into the closet. And Sharon, my sister-in-law, says, Hey Lauren. Who are you talking to? and Lauren says, It's my friend, Jenny.

Sharon knew it wasn't uncommon for children Lauren's age to have imaginary friends, so she wasn't overly concerned about her daughter at first. But when Lauren started repeating some of the things that Jenny was telling her, she soon became alarmed. Jenny, it seemed, was a little Native American girl, and she didn't like any of the grown-ups. She only liked Lauren. When asked why Jenny didn't like grown-ups, Lauren replied it was because they were white men, and white men had murdered Jenny and her whole family. This was highly upsetting to Sharon. How was Lauren coming up with such things? She wondered if her daughter might be going crazy, so she told her husband, Rob's brother, who researched the property and found that two hundred years previously, this particular bit of land in Brownstown, Michigan, had been inhabited by Native Americans until the settlers came and massacred them all, and that the house was actually built on top of their old burial grounds. Knowing this, and in an effort to keep their daughter away from the entity, Rob's brother and his family sold the house and moved away. Later, when one of his brother's neighborhood friends called him to ask why they had moved, he was reluctant to answer, until his neighbor asked if it was because of the ghosts. Everyone in the neighborhood, he was told, was having similar problems. While the move turned out successfully for his brother and his family, this apparition, Jenny, wasn't to be so easily dismissed, at least not for Rob. It continued to plague him.

"It's pretty creepy where I currently live," he told me. "When I go to bed, I normally sleep with the door open. Six or seven months ago, I shut my bedroom door for some reason, and I went to sleep. The sound of the door opening woke me up. I looked and the door was open six to eight inches, and I saw a figure of what looked like my niece, all grown up now, standing in the doorway. You know, it's about five foot, three inches, long hair, can't see the face. So I jumped up, and all of a sudden, the shadow disappeared. The door didn't even shut. It just disappeared. So I went through my entire house and made sure there was no one there and all the doors and windows were shut. Then I went back to sleep. I woke up at 4:30 a.m. and the door opened again, and there's the same figure standing there looking at me. So I jumped up and raced for the door but, just like before, the figure just faded away before I could reach the door."

Then, just as Rob was reaching for the doorknob, the door suddenly shut all on its own. He put his hand on the knob and pulled it but couldn't get the door to open. It was stuck. After a few seconds, he finally succeeded in opening the door but, again, there was no one on the other side. Another check of his house turned up nothing out of the ordinary. The doors and windows were still secured. He could think of nothing else to do, so he called his niece. After expressing surprise that her uncle was calling so early in the morning, she emphatically stated that she had not just been in his house.

It reminded him so much of what happened at his brother's old house on the Indian burial ground. "I can't help but feel that this thing has somehow attached itself to me. And that's not all. About a year earlier, as I was sitting in my recliner watching television, I noticed a dark gray-colored mist in the hallway. It's hovering about six inches off the ground, and then it starts coming toward me. Now I'm wide awake watching TV, so I go to get up and see what this is. I thought there might be a fire somewhere in the house or something, you know? So I try to get up from the recliner but suddenly, I can't move my arms or legs. I'm paralyzed. This mist is rolling towards me now, and I can't move a muscle, only my eyes. This thing approaches and starts circling around my chair, and all I can do is move my eyeballs back and forth, watching it. I can see the TV. I see exactly what I'm watching. I know that I'm not dreaming but I don't know what this thing is, and I'm very scared because I can't move. I'm frozen."

After a few minutes, which seemed like forever to Rob, whatever the mist was went away. Afterward, he spoke to someone about doing a cleansing of the house but kept putting it off. Then a few days later, it happened again. "This time," Rob began, "I started saying the Lord's Prayer when I felt the paralysis come over me. I still couldn't move for a minute or so, but it didn't prolong itself this time. Both the feeling of being paralyzed and the misty figure went away very quickly. I believe in God, but you know what I did then? The next day I went to the person I had contacted earlier and got everything I needed to cleanse my house. I've not had that problem since."

Rob has also concluded that all of these incidents are related and that there must be some reason behind all of these things. He realizes this now, after several years of research, but just like most of us, didn't have a clue in the beginning. What *was* the beginning for Rob Karnafel, you might ask. As it turns out, just before he started seeing the ghosts as a child, he saw something else.

When he was seven years old, he saw a flying saucer, Rob told me. His mom was with him, and she called it a flying machine. "I didn't know what it was. I said that it looked like the spaceship from the television show, *Lost in Space*. Other people had seen it too, I guess. When my dad came home, we told him about it and then he turned on the TV and there they were talking about it all over the news and he said, 'I'll be damned! You really did see a flying saucer.' A little later that year we went to our family cottage, and in the room where me and my brother would sleep there is this big day window. Every night around midnight the moon would come up and illuminate the whole bedroom. I remember it like it was yesterday. We had this Mickey Mouse clock on the wall, you know, with the big white hands, and every night, the hands would be almost to twelve by the time we made it to bed. Every night, the moonlight on the clock would be covered by this big shadow standing at the window. Whatever it was, you could tell it was looking in, but it would just stand there for a few minutes, watching us, I guess. Then it would move away. That happened every time we went up there to the cottage until about the age of nine. I've seen things pretty much throughout my life and didn't realize it until I started studying all of this."

These days, the paranormal activity in Rob's home continues, just as he continues his quest for answers regarding all the things which officially do not exist. He has started a YouTube podcast called *Brunch With Bigfoot Michigan Rob*, where he interviews eyewitnesses to unexplained phenomena.

3

Unholy Alliances – Ann's Story

"Never in my entire life did I ever think that I would see a Bigfoot," Ann Selene, author of *Aperture in the Veil: Born into a Preternatural World*, told me when I spoke to her in 2022. This is surprising, since she claims to have been beset by the more preternatural aspects of this world since infancy. She didn't think much about the Bigfoot phenomenon, having had no experience with it before, and when she thought of it at all, she felt sure that the creatures, if they existed, were merely part of the natural world. A yet undiscovered and extremely rare part, yes, but still as natural an animal as a deer or a bear. She certainly never expected to encounter one herself. But that's exactly what happened to her and her group one night back in the summer of 2020 while on a ghost hunting expedition at a remote cemetery in Minerva, Ohio. They were calling for spirits using a spirit box, and Bigfoot answered! But before we investigate that experience, a cursory look at Ms. Selene's past is definitely warranted here.

Some of her first memories were from when she was a baby lying in her crib, she told me. She remembers watching a shadow entity peering at her from outside her door and wrapping its long, dark fingers around the doorjamb. She would also see darkly cloaked and hooded figures watching her from the shadows at times. These shadow figures, as well as other poltergeist activities, would follow Ann the rest of her life, even when she went to visit relatives as an adult. One night, as she was staying with her sister, Lynn, they both awoke from sleep and were startled to see a cloaked, hooded figure standing at the foot of their beds. Both Ann and her sister have children, and they tried to shield the kids from these paranormal visitations until the kids started seeing the shadow people themselves, at which point the situation could no longer be kept hidden.

Objects would often move on their own in Ann's home. Loud banging sounds on the floors would awaken them from sleep. Apparitions would sometimes appear to Ann, who managed to get a photograph of one to include in her book. She strongly believes in reincarnation, mostly due to what she believes are past-life memories from several incarnations on this plane of existence. And as with other witnesses, the UFO phenomenon is also connected to this one as well.

Ann was born and raised in Oregon, the daughter

of an Air Force military man, who taught her how to spot flying saucers back when she was a young girl. When she was nine years old, she witnessed two UFOs. One was V-shaped with blinking lights of varying colors, and the other was a solid silver disc-shaped object. They both streaked away as she was watching, so quickly that her eyes could not follow. When I questioned her further about her dad, she disclosed that he knew all about the existence of the unknown craft and that there were many secret underground facilities he knew of as well, but he wasn't allowed to talk to anyone about those subjects. His top-secret clearance could be revoked, and he would lose his job—or worse—so he never spoke too much about them to his daughter or his wife. Ann told me of an abduction dream she'd had just before giving birth to her first child. She was in the hospital waiting to deliver her daughter when a nurse walked into her room late that night. She watched as the nurse approached her bed, then took a pair of scissors from her pocket and cut off Ann's hospital armbands. When Ann protested, the "nurse" said nothing in reply but walked over to the side of her bed and injected something into her IV unit, causing Ann to go almost immediately to sleep. When she awoke the next morning, she had injection marks on her arm, and when the morning nurse came in, she scolded Ann for removing her armbands. She hadn't removed them, she told the nurse. It was the nurse who came into her room last night who cut them off her wrist. The woman responded that no other nurse had visited her room the previous night, so it had to have been her. In addition, she has also awoken to find herself wearing different clothes than when she went to sleep and claims that she and all three of her children experienced missing time one evening in February 2022.

As we see here, spiritual phenomena have always been with Ann, who considers herself a spiritual person, awake and acutely aware of the reality of the paranormal. She has pursued her interest in contacting spirits for several years. So it was no surprise to find her standing there in the Ohio cemetery with several of her friends in 2020, trying to use a spirit box to connect with the souls of the dead.

"We were using what's called the Estes Method," Ann recounted. "You have noise-canceling headphones, and you have a blindfold. You pick one person who puts those on, and then you turn on the spirit box and just listen through the static. You hear words as you're listening to this, and you just call out the words you hear. The other people in the group ask questions out loud, and the person will essentially be answering back through whatever energy or spirit being that is able to use that to speak to us. Everything, every answer we were getting back, seemed to be about the land, or it was very connected to the land and, according to the girl wearing the blindfold, was given in a very sing-songy kind of voice that would seem to go around in circles, then trail off into random words. She got the impression of a deer-headed entity, complete with antlers, and the word *trickster* immediately came to everyone's mind at that moment. And because there were forests all around us, I had the bright idea to hold a session deep inside the woods."

So off they went to do just that, despite the lateness of the hour. They loaded their equipment into a vehicle and struck out for the woods. Ann describes herself as a "sensitive" and felt an overwhelming energy once they had arrived at a suitable spot deep in the forest. In the forests of the Pacific Northwest, things were quiet, she told me, but there in Ohio it was like an orchestra. Looking back, she said that she didn't take note of it at the time, but probably should have.

Indeed but as they say hindsight is 20/20.

After the group had all their ghost hunting equipment set up, the began settling down while making plans when Ann began to hear footsteps coming from the darkness of the woods to her right. "The footsteps sounded very distinct," she said. "I could tell that whatever was taking the steps was bipedal, and I'm also thinking, 'Okay, it's nighttime. You're just scared. It's likely just a rabbit or a bird.' I sit there a few seconds longer and I hear this really low, guttural growl. It was so low that I felt it in my chest. It was so terrifying that I thought I was going to die. I felt physically sick. But I look around at my group and, strangely, no one is reacting at all to any of this. It was as if I was the only one hearing the noises, so I thought that it had to just be me. So I stand up and I grab a flashlight, and now I'm facing the area that was behind me, and I have my flashlight and I'm looking. I don't really see anything until I go over to the opposite direction, and just out of the flashlight's reach, I can see the silhouette. And it was the head and the shoulder and the arm, and I'm just staring at it and I'm like, 'I'm not here for you. I'm not here for this.'"

Feeling extremely uncomfortable, Ann took the flashlight off the tree and turned away. Just then, they all heard what sounded like an extremely loud, open-handed smack to their vehicle. After a quick search didn't turn up anything, Ann stated that she had to leave that place, to get out of there. She hadn't told anyone what she'd seen at that point, and what she'd seen had really shaken her up. She glanced again at the tree where the figure had been standing, but there was nothing there. She quickly explained to everyone what she'd witnessed as they gathered up their gear, loaded it into the vehicle, and headed out of the woods and down into a nearby field just below a forested ridge that they decided would make a good base camp.

After they struck camp, Ann tried to calm down. She was used to paranormal investigations, but this was something else altogether. Had she really seen a Bigfoot creature? The idea was just incredible to her. After a couple of hours had passed, they decided to break out the spirit box again. Again, the spirit box spoke of the land and the connection the beings who were speaking had to it. Also, they claimed that they were only a myth now but were once worshipped as gods. Then, according to Ann, it seemed like something else started coming through the spirit box. A different entity. One with a keen interest in their children.

Suddenly, they could hear movement coming down toward them from atop the ridge. "There's a ridge and there's a street" she said, "and the moonlight was shining behind the branches. The same silhouette that I saw earlier was right there. The head. The shoulders. And I wasn't the only one that saw it. It was kind of moving back and forth in the moonlight." The person wearing the blindfold and headphones then said, "See? You see me." And they could see it, all right. When the spirit that was speaking through the box began to disclose personal information about the kids, private information that only the parents themselves would know, such as their nicknames, they decided to end the session. They set out a blanket in the field, and it was then that a member of the party decided to play an audio recording of an alleged Bigfoot vocalization taken twenty years ago in Ohio in 1994.

That proved to be a mistake.

When they had all heard what sounded like a loud,

open-handed smack on one of the vehicles earlier in the evening, everyone was perplexed as to what might have made the noise, but there was absolutely no mistaking the sound that reverberated through the woods this time. "I'm telling you, the sound that came out of those woods," Ann said. "It was terrifying. It was the exact same sound, same tone, same cadence—everything, as the Ohio [Bigfoot] recording that my friend had just played, only about ten times louder. We all just froze, and I just stood there terrified. I'd never once in my life thought that I would hear something like this or see Bigfoot. I never thought that I would experience anything like that. So we're all standing there frozen, and that's when we hear what sounds like something ripping a tree out of the ground and smacking it hard against another tree."

The calamitous racket startled everyone from their catharsis, and they wasted no time in hurrying to their vehicles and beating a hasty retreat out of there. "I guess you could say that I believed in Bigfoot before then," she said. "I never discounted those who said they had experiences. I just didn't think it was for me. I never needed to look for it. I never needed to search. I just didn't think much about it before then. Let me tell you, I went from a believer to a knower that night."

It's quite telling that the Bigfoot creatures (as she felt strongly that there were more than one of them involved in the occurrence) successfully communicated with Ann's group by means of a device intended to communicate with spirits of the dead. As of this writing, Ann and her family are still contending with the frequent disruptions in their daily lives caused by unseen, or ghostly, phenomena. Cabinet doors open by themselves, electronics seldom work as they should, and spectral sounds emanating from somewhere in the house are common occurrences. In February of 2022, Ann and all three of her kids experienced an episode of missing time while playing a family board game in her home.

When asked what she thinks these Bigfoot creatures might be, she said that she honestly doesn't know for sure—perhaps some kind of nature elemental or something along those lines. One thing she was sure of, however, was the apparent interconnectivity between these creatures and the spirit world. How else can you explain it when you're calling for spirits of the dead – and Bigfoot answers?

4

A Plethora of High Strangeness
– Darrell's Story

Darrell Denton is one of the most highly regarded, respected men in the state of Tennessee. After he graduated college in the late seventies, he went into local politics where he spent the next twenty-six years, first as alderman for Ridgetop, Tennessee (in Robertson County), then as commissioner and later as mayor. He was a different kind of politician who did things his way, the right way, and never let his integrity become compromised for love nor money. Darrell was kind and fair to everyone, honest to a fault, and he soon found himself at the very top of his social class. He had money, lots of cars, and property, and his everyday friends that he hung out with were mostly highly successful movie and television personalities, sports celebrities, and country music stars of the time making big waves just sixteen miles away in Nashville.

But Darrell had a secret, one that very few people

knew about. In fact, he had a few of them. He had experienced some strange things in his life. He was a witness to things that might sound a bit crazy to "ordinary" folks. Would people have looked at him differently had they known? Perhaps, but some people are not as wise as others.

At heart Darrell was and still is a good old salt-of-the-earth, down-home country boy. And, like most other country boys, deer hunting was a way of life for him and his family and friends. But the morning of November 6th, 1992, on his grandfather's farm in Cannon County, that all changed.

His grandfather had a large 250-acre farm mostly covered in dense hardwood forests and pastureland and had lived there his entire life. This was the preferred hunting location for Darrell and his friends, and they had hunted there for several years already with good results and no problems. But opening day would turn a dream location into a nightmare. In fact, that cold morning, standing in his deer stand twenty-five feet off the ground, would change Darrell's life forever and completely alter his perspective about what was real, not myth, in this amazingly mysterious world.

First Encounter

I was more scared than I've ever been in my life. I didn't even know I had that kind of fear in me, to be honest. But I sure did. It was November 6th of 1992. Every year me and three of my friends would take my camper. I had a camper I pulled behind my truck, and they'd follow behind in their trucks. We all had four wheelers, and they had them in the trucks. We would go to my grandfather's farm in Cannon County, Tennessee, which was about ninety miles from where I lived at the time, and we would pull the camper up next to his barn and set up camp. He had electricity in the barn, and we would plug that up where all our lights in the camper would work. We would be there that whole week of opening day of black powder or, as we called it, muzzle-loader season. In Tennessee it would last a week, and we would always be up there that whole opening week because it was a really good place to hunt. My grandfather had a large farm, and it was extremely rural. Isolated. Heavily forested with just acres and acres of old-growth timber— no neighbors for a good long distance.

My grandfather, D. W. Sauls, at that time, lived by himself. My grandmother was still living, but she had moved into an apartment in town. She'd wanted all the finer conveniences of modern life and my grandpa didn't care about any of them, so he lived on the farm by himself. He never even owned a car. He had a mule and a couple of wagons that he would take to town, and I would get to ride with him when I was a kid on Saturdays into town to get groceries. After we had moved to Richtown prior to that, we would visit quite often. We were very close.

So every year me and three of my buddies would drive up to my grandfather's farm, 250 acres of dense hardwood forests and rolling pastures, to deer hunt, and we would camp out that whole week. Camp out, grill out and, you know, just have a good time while we hunt. We all had different spots we went to. We had several deer blinds that were previously built from a couple years before, and we would carry climbing stands, which you carried on your back, and you can put it around a tree and climb up it and hunt from a tree if you preferred to do that.

We set up camp the day before the season opened, and after I had gone up to my grandfather's house, he and I began speaking. My grandfather was really close to me. He was ninety-two years old at the time, but he was in tremendous shape and tremendous health. Most people thought he was a lot younger because he looked it and acted it. So I asked him. 'Granddad, I want to hunt somewhere different this time. Where would be the best place to go to get a trophy deer this year because I want a big, large rack to hang on my wall?' We were standing on his back porch, and he pointed out over the hills and said, 'Boy.' He never called me by my name. Just 'Boy.' I don't know why, but I had thirteen cousins, and he called them all 'Boy.' That's what he called me too, even though out of all my siblings and cousins, he and I were the closest. My grandmother, too, because I had lived with them when I was just a kid. But, he said, 'Boy, you see that third hill way over yonder?' And I said, 'Yes, Granddad,' And he said, 'That's where I would go 'cause nobody ever goes back in there.' And he told me, 'You and I have been back in there before. That's my old home place. That old house I grew up in is in there. It's fallin' in now, but you can still see part of the chimney and tin roof. I would go to that holler and hunt in that area if I was you. Ain't nobody been in there in many a year.'

I had never hunted in the area he was pointing to, myself, which was a good forty-five minutes to an hour's walk from the house, I reckoned. I had always hunted close to the farm or within walking distance of his house or our campsite. We had lots of steep hills and hollers there. Bluffs, mountains, and hills so steep you'd have to climb them to get up there. This was miles away from other homes. There were lots of farms, but there was a great distance between homes where other people lived. So, I said, 'Okay, I'll do that, Granddad. That's where I'll hunt in the morning.'

My other buddies had already left to go find their hunting spots, either in the existing stands or they were carrying their own stands on their backs like I was, so I walked on over there, through his back yard, which led into a big sage field that was about two hundred yards wide to the wood line. You had to go through a gate before you could enter the sage field. So I lifted up the latch and went through into the field, walked across it to the barbed-wire fence that went into the woods. My grandfather kept cattle in that area at one time. So I climbed over the barbed-wire fence and went up this real steep hill. I climbed that first hill and went over it, down the other side to the bottom. There was an old, fallen-down section of fence, so I stepped over that. There hadn't been any cattle there for years. I went over the second hill and down to the bottom of it. By the time I got to the top of that third hill, it seemed a very long walk—at least an hour from where I started.

I could see from the top of that hill the area where the

old homesite was. It was wooded over with hardwoods, but it wasn't real thick, and the leaves were off the trees. Going down that hill, I had to cross over a little bluff and a gulley to get down to a place where I could see the actual spot where the remains of the house was located and, in doing that, I had walked along the creek edge and saw a tree up on the side of the hill that looked like the perfect spot. It was right next to a large, and I mean long, large and tall cane thicket. The gray cane shoots were about twelve to fifteen feet tall and growing thick all the way down the side of the creek. I found my spot there and the tree overlooking the creek that I'd picked out and walked across the creek and up into the clearing at the bottom. Then, I carefully climbed the tree and put my deer stand up about twenty feet off the ground. When I had climbed back down, I walked around the area looking for deer signs and, to my delight, there was deer sign everywhere along the creek: tracks, tree rubs, and scrapes. You could easily see where a lot of animals had been steadily traveling up and down it.

There was a tree limb that I jumped up and grabbed and pulled down, and I had a drag rag tied around my boot, which is a rag soaked in the scent of a female deer in heat, to cover up my own scent. I took the rag and wrapped it around the end of the limb and let the limb go. It bounced back up to about ten feet, just low enough to let the aroma drift down the holler. So I crossed back over the creek and climbed back up into my stand. I trimmed off a few branches, which allowed me to have a better line of sight down to the creek and to hang up my lunch and a pack filled with extra powder horns and powder that I would be carrying the next day. After everything was ready, I climbed back down and made my way back to Granddad's place.

That night would be spent watching his buddies having a beer or two (Darrell didn't drink) while sitting around a roaring fire, enjoying good company and good conversation, eagerly anticipating a successful morning hunt. All four men turned in early to get a good night's rest before the hunt began.

For Darrell, it would be the last good night's sleep he would enjoy for seven years.

Granddad always got up at 4:00 a.m., no matter what. At about 4:05, he knocked on the camper door and hollered, "Boy! Time to get up."

So, we all got up and got ready, and I headed off in the direction of the sage field carrying my light, gun, and my equipment. I got across the field and made it to the wood line, and I crossed over the barbed-wire fence, making my way just as I had the day before and trying not to use my flashlight whenever possible as I didn't want to make my presence known to any deer that might be in the area. When I was making my way up the second hill, in complete darkness, I heard something that sounded like someone was walking through the forest to my left, not far from where I was standing. I stopped to listen. It didn't sound like an animal or a small critter or anything like that, but something much heavier, and I thought that maybe someone's cow had gotten loose and made it onto my grandfather's property. I didn't want to do it, but I shined the light over to the left at the noise but couldn't see anything, which I thought was odd considering the proximity of the noises. I walked a little further and crossed up onto the third and last hill. I crossed the spot where the last fence was, and I could still hear something walking over there, so I stopped. And it stopped. When I walked again, it walked also and, every time that I stopped, whatever was in the woods would stop also. Whatever it was, it didn't behave like any other animal that I'd ever seen or heard of in the woods before.

At that point, I started to get a little nervous thinking that somebody was here hunting in my area, or that I was hunting in his area, but I couldn't quite make sense out of it because I knew that my grandfather had never given anyone permission to hunt his land except for me and my three friends, and he'd told me specifically that no one had been back this way for years and years. Anyway, I went on down and I had a hard time finding my tree stand. It was so dark. I couldn't find it, so I walked along the edge of the creek with my flashlight and followed it down a way and, luckily, it ran right into my stand. Everything looks so much different at night than it does in the daytime, especially when you're not familiar with the area. I was anxious to get up and into my stand and a bit nervous because I knew that something, or someone, was still in the area with me.

I climbed up into my stand and got set. I'm guessing it was about five-thirty in the morning. I got all my stuff hanging from the limbs, got out my binoculars, and sat back. My stand had a little bar that goes around in front of you that you can lay your gun on, and a little camouflage drape that unsnaps and rolls down to cover your legs. I let that down and I'm sitting there, completely camouflaged, and wearing black under my eyes so the sun doesn't glimmer off my skin when it comes up, the whole nine yards. And I didn't hear anything except for the walking sounds coming up from my left. I heard something that sounded like larger footsteps, just a few of them going down to my left, and then they just stopped. I was glad the noises had stopped and didn't think much more about it as I sat there while the sun came up, and the creek had a lot of fog coming off it that morning. I remember that very well and what a bright, sunny, beautiful morning it was as I sat up in the hardwoods.

I could see the fog coming off the creek and starting to see signs that the woods were springing to life. The squirrels and rabbits were beginning to stir and move around. It was a very peaceful scene. At around seven or seven-thirty, three deer came from somewhere in the big cane thicket to my left. I saw the first one walk across the creek to the other side of the game trail, a doe. Then two more does, smaller ones, followed it, walked across the trail in front of me, and started milling around trying to find acorns and such, looking for something to eat. The bigger doe was to my left, the smaller ones to my right. I watched them for about fifteen to twenty minutes. I figured the bigger one was the momma of the two smaller ones.

Then, all of a sudden, the momma doe's ears stood straight up, and it looked over to the cane thicket area to my left. Then the other deer stopped moving. Their ears went up, too, and they all started staring in the same direction. Then, the momma deer lifted her head up like she was sniffing the air, stomped her right foot on the ground, and made a real loud blowing noise like deer are known to do. I got excited then thinking that any second a big trophy buck was going to come into the picture looking to rut with the doe.

But that's not what happened at all. After the deer made the blowing noise, she stared one more time at the thicket, then turned and bolted off to my right as fast as she could go across the creek in front of me, immediately followed by the two smaller deer. It was like somebody had shot at them. Deer don't normally act like that unless something has spooked them, or they're frightened by something. I sat there for another five minutes or so, and nothing happened, and I thought, "Well . . . that's mighty peculiar."

And it sure was a fine morning for animals to

be acting peculiarly around old Granddad's place, it seemed. A fine morning, indeed.

So here I am thinking that a buck would come out hot any second, chasing after the does because that's what they were running from and, after about five minutes, I saw that the canes in the middle of the cane thicket to my left were moving. This was tall cane, twelve to fifteen feet or so, and real thick. Way too thick to see inside it, it was so bunched together. And I thought, 'Wow! This must be a really big deer to make the cane shoots move like that." I watched the canes move the rest of the way through the thicket, and when it got to the edge next to the stream, out steps this huge, black creature—this monster. I thought, 'What in the world?' I couldn't believe what my eyes were seeing. I kept staring at it thinking, "What is that? I can't be seeing this."

Keep in mind that Darrell is a big guy. Despite his pleasant, humble demeanor, at six feet, five inches tall and weighing 275 pounds, he has never been the type to be intimidated or scared by anyone or anything. Despite this fact, he felt the blood in his veins run cold as he silently watched the thing. This creature was huge, standing on two legs like a man and covered in thick, jet-black hair. It took one step forward, then leaped completely across the ten-to-twelve-foot-wide creek in one jump and landed on the other side of the creek bank on the game trail. It walked right down straight in front of him on that game trail and stopped next to the drag rag that he had hung in the tree. Then it looked up straight up at him twenty-five feet up in his stand.

Now Darrell could get a good, unobstructed look at the thing from only around fifty feet away. He could see the monster clearly from head to toe, and what he saw filled him with terror. In was humanlike, though covered from head to toe in short, jet-black hair. It had a human-shaped head and black, leathery-looking skin on its sparsely covered, wrinkled forehead, a flat nose, and dark black eyes. Its large mouth was twisted up on the right side into a disturbing-looking grimace. According to Darrell, the thing's face looked mean, evil, like it wanted nothing more than to reach up, grab him out of his stand, and kill him. The most evil-looking face you can imagine, he told me. It had a thick, short neck, big chest, and four-foot-wide shoulders. Its forearms and hands looked somewhat overly large, he said. The hands were human, with black, untrimmed fingernails. The creature's thighs were massive, he further described, but from the knees down the legs looked somewhat skinny to him. The feet were very large, with square, black toenails, as if they had been trimmed or worn away from walking in the woods. He could clearly see from the thing's sex organs, which looked like a normal human's in proportion to its body, that it was most definitely a male. He estimated the creature's weight at around eight hundred pounds.

By this time, I was basically just frozen. I thought, "What do I do here?" I have one shot with a .50 caliber muzzle-loader. I had both hands on my gun that was leaning against the safety bar that went around me. I thought no way if I shot the thing the bullet would take this huge creature down, and if it didn't, I was done for.

The two subjects stared at each other for ten to fifteen full minutes, which must have felt like three eternities to Darrell, then it showed the witness its teeth, and that's when the fear inside doubled. It didn't have fangs, Darrell said, just regular, flat teeth that looked stained and yellow. It looked at him, showed its teeth and then growled. That growl that it let out. I can still feel it in my chest right now to this day.

Darrell paused reflectively here. I get cold chills telling this story sometimes even to this day. And it's been over thirty years since it happened. I was so scared when that monster looked at me and growled like that, low and deep and loud. So low and powerful you can feel it in your bones. I call it a monster because that's what it looked like to me: a monster. I had never been that scared before. I didn't even know I had that kind of fear in me. I could barely even breathe. I thought sure it was gonna come across the creek and yank me down out of that tree.

I know it was eight feet tall because it reached up and grabbed that drag rag, smelled of it. Then it just ripped the whole limb the rag was on right out of the tree and threw it on the ground. The limb wasn't massive, about three or four inches around but, still, it must have taken a tremendous amount of strength to tear that whole limb off. Then it took two steps back to where it was standing, turned, looked at me again with the meanest, maddest look I've ever seen, like it wanted to kill me, and lets out the most ungodly, loudest scream—roar—that I've heard before or since. I'm telling you, it shook me. I was terrified. Since then, I listened to a lot of supposed Bigfoot vocalizations, but I ain't never heard anything like the scream this thing made that day. It echoed all down the holler, and I thought, "Well, this is it. Do I shoot? Do I run? Can I run?" I was just stunned. I remember looking down at my watch. It was exactly 8:23 a.m. when this happened.

Then, much to Darrell's relief, the creature turned and started walking away. It turned to look at him one last time, then continued into the hardwoods and out of sight. When that thing was out of sight, I had just one thought on my mind: that it would take way too long for me to climb down out of that tree. So, I just lowered the safety bar in front of me, held my gun up above my head and jumped down out of that tree stand. It was a good twenty to twenty-five feet up, and I hit the leaves, sliding and rolling all the way down the creek bank and into the creek.

He jumped up out of the creek and ran as fast as he could in the opposite direction of the creature, back toward the farm, abandoning his deer stand and all his extra gear without even a second thought. As he ran, he glanced back behind him to make sure the thing wasn't following him. He ran like a deer up and over that first hill. Halfway to the top of the second hill, he turned and looked back again, and there, standing on top of the hill he'd just retreated from, was the creature, or another one that resembled it, watching him as he ran away.

Seeing it gave me even more adrenaline. So I ran

faster than I've ever ran before in my life over that second hill. And it's still there. I don't know if it was the same creature as it was heading in the opposite direction of me when I lit out of there. It could've been another one, but it looked just like it. I can still remember how hard and fast my heart was beating in my chest as I ran, like a trip hammer. By the time I got to the top of that third hill, I was running so fast that I just jumped over that six-foot-tall, barbed-wire fence. Stopping to climb over it wasn't even an option. Unfortunately, my left pant leg got caught on the top strand of barb wire and it ripped my pant leg off up to my knee and put a big gash in my leg. That didn't slow me down one bit. I didn't even think about it. I was still running. I don't even remember getting up off the ground, just running like a wild horse across that big sage field to the gate. I opened it up and looked behind me again. There was nothing there, but that didn't matter much to me at that point. I latched the gate and ran like hell up onto my granddad's porch, opened the back door up and got inside, then slammed it back shut. I looked out the window of the door and didn't see it anywhere, thank God.

I walked into the living room where Granddad was sitting in his rocking chair in front of an old potbellied, wood-burning stove that he had stoked up in the corner, and just plopped down onto the floor beside the stove, bleeding and gasping for breath. I didn't think I was ever going to catch my breath from running so hard. Granddad just looked down at me, unalarmed, and said,

"Boy, what's wrong with you?" It took me a few seconds before I could say anything, but finally I said, "Granddad, I seen a monster in your woods." And he said, "A what?" and I said, "Yes! A monster! I've never seen anything that looked like that around here before!" Then, he asked me what it looked like, and I told him. He had me repeat it again to be sure, then rather nonchalantly said, "Oh, you seen a Wood Booger."

Darrell was taken aback. He'd never heard of a Wood Booger before. In all these years, his grandfather had never spoken of them a single time. "What, Granddad?", he asked."What in the heck is a Wood Booger?"

"Well, Boy," his grandfather began. "Them things been around here all my life. I've seen four of them in my life, so far. I'd be working in one of the fields and look up and there'd be one over in the trees watching me work. They never tried to harm me or anybody I heard tell of. I do still hear them a lot in the woods, mostly at night."

I still could hardly believe what I was hearing. Why in the world didn't you ever tell me about those things?

"Well, you grew up here on this farm," Grandpa told me. "You hunted and camped here all by yourself in these woods plum back to when you was a youngin. Remember the nights you and your friends used to stay out in the hayloft all night in that old barn? I didn't want y'all to not have any fun and be yourselves. I didn't want you to be scared because I don't think they would ever harm anyone."

Well, if I had known there was one of *those* things out there, I never would've gone out in those woods a single time. Ever.

My granddad chuckled. "Remember all those times your grandma would tell you at night to get inside the house or the Booger Man would get you? Well, she was talking about the Wood Boogers."

I can't believe you've known about these things all these years, I said, shaking my head.

"Yeah, Boy. And there's more than just one of 'em. My grandfather, your great-great-grandfather, had a big old log henhouse right beside his house, and it had been there for years already. And he told me that sometimes, during the coldest winters, these things would get hungry and go into the henhouse and take two or three chickens. They wouldn't take 'em all. Just some of 'em, and they'd leave a little pile of sticks and rocks like they was paying for the chickens. Said they'd done it for many years, and they never tried to hurt nobody. You probably interrupted their hunt. Pappy told me that they were territorial, and you *were* in their area. I really didn't even think about 'em being in there, but you don't need to be scared of 'em, Boy. I think you'll be all right."

Despite his granddad's advice, Darrell never went into those woods again in his life. He was sitting right there at the house when his buddies got back. One of them had killed a nice buck. He asked them, since they'd all been hunting there a few years already, if any of them had ever seen or heard anything strange in the woods while they were hunting. They didn't know what he was talking about. When he told them what had happened to him and what he saw, they all laughed, so he just let it go. Regardless, he spent the rest of the week inside his granddad's house while his other three friends continued to hunt. He wouldn't even sleep out in his camper with the rest of the guys, choosing instead to sleep in the house where he felt safe. He was done with hunting. He didn't care anything about it anymore, knowing those things were out there in the woods, he told me.

It was a life-changing experience. It changed my whole perspective on being in the woods with a gun and thinking that you're at the very top of the food chain when really, you're not. I had nightmares for years after that. It was seven years before I could bring myself to go back into the woods by myself again. Looking back on it now, I don't think that it wanted to kill me. It could have if it had wanted to. I was there up in that tree with no way to get down and away. It wanted to scare me and run me out of the area. Which it did, all right. It's been over thirty years, and I still have no intention of ever setting foot there again.

I still think about that day. Hardly a day has gone by that I didn't think of it. To this day, I never completely got over that. Not really. I don't think I would've *ever* gotten over it at all if it wasn't for my second experience. That really changed my outlook on at least some of these creatures.

Second Encounter

In March 1999, seven years after that first terrifying encounter, Darrell finally got up enough courage to go fishing by himself again at one of his family's lifelong fishing spots on the Cumberland River, just outside of Nashville, Tennessee. He parked behind a water/ sewage treatment plant, grabbed his fishing poles and gear, which consisted of a minnow bucket with four dozen minnows and a tackle box that he carried down in a five-gallon bucket, and walked down to a gate located at the far edge of the property. The area was off limits to the public, but one of his best friends' dads had worked there for a long time and had shown them the place many years before. This was a favored spot to catch some nice slab crappie, and it had been way too long since he had wet a line.

After opening and shutting the gate behind him, he started out on a small game trail through the woods and walked a couple hundred yards through the woods to his spot on the river. He went with some trepidation due to his experience with the creature seven years previously, but this was a place with which he was well familiar, and he had never seen or heard anything out of the ordinary here. Besides, he thought to himself, his grandfather's farm was nearly one hundred miles away from here.

Those woods went on for miles and miles along the river. It was really grown up and thick back in there. Our spot had a creek running right next to it that emptied into the river, and there was a sand bar that ran from the edge of the banks all the way out to the middle of the river. When the water was at normal levels, you could walk out onto that sand bar and reel your fish in because if you didn't, you would get your line hung up in all the branches and roots growing out of the riverbank there. I took my minnow bucket and tackle box out, then turned the five-gallon bucket upside down next to a tree and used it as a seat. I caught a fish, a keeper, and I went down and put it on the stringer, which was attached to the side of the riverbank, then walked up and sat back down. I'd put the bait bucket right beside me on my left and I reached into it, grabbed another minnow, rebaited my hook, and cast it back out. I sat there for a while until I caught another fish. I went and put it on the stringer, sat back down and reached for my minnow bucket for another minnow—but it was gone. I thought, "What the heck?" So, I looked around everywhere, in the water, on the bank, but I couldn't find it anywhere, and I thought "How in the heck do you lose a minnow bucket in the middle of the woods with no one else around?" There was an area of thick kudzu vines to my left, kinda like ivy-looking stuff, and it went all the way down the riverbank, and there was a small trail that went through there. It was overgrown with limbs and brush, and you had to get down on your hands and knees to get through there. I got down and went down that trail just a little way, maybe ten feet, and I didn't see my bucket, so I gathered up my stuff and left thinking that someone had played a joke on me and took my bait, ruining my day.

A week later, Darrell returned once again, alone and carrying a brand-new minnow bucket. It was a cloudy day, and it had been raining the day before. Both the river and the creek were higher than the previous week, forcing Darrell to fish six or seven feet higher up on the bank. The sandbar was underwater now and was no longer visible. He set out his fishing lines, secured his stringer to the bank, and got settled down, once again setting his five-gallon bucket up next to a tree with his minnow bucket down beside him on his left-hand side toward the tangled growth of kudzu vines and game trail. He noticed that the trail was muddy now, with deer and other animal tracks evident from where he was sitting.

It wasn't too long before he caught his first fish on one of his lines, and he walked down to retrieve the catch. After he caught the fish, he put it on the stringer and went and sat back down, and just like before, his minnow bucket was gone again.

Highly puzzled and annoyed and thinking that, surely, someone must live nearby or that his friends were somehow to blame, he began another search of the immediate area. After all, minnow buckets didn't just vanish into thin air, and whoever was responsible was putting a serious damper on his recent fishing trips. HeI looked all around. It wasn't floating in the river. It was kind of windy that day, he said. A storm was moving in, but the wind hadn't blown the bucket into the river. Those Styrofoam buckets don't sink easily. I didn't see it nowhere, and I didn't know what to think. Who in the world would be taking my darn bait buckets? It didn't make any sense but, once again, I didn't have any bait, so I gathered up my gear, let the fish off the stringer, and left again feeling a little defeated and mad.

Losing the two bait buckets like that weighed heavily on his mind at home. That next weekend, he returned. This time, he tied twenty feet of white nylon string to the handle of his minnow bucket and secured the other end to the tree next to where he was sitting. He had a good day that day, landing several nice fish almost immediately. The water was back to normal levels now, and when another fish sank his bobber, he grabbed the pole and walked out onto the sandbar to reel it in without any trouble. He put the fish on the stringer and walked back up to his spot and, sure enough, his minnow bucket was nowhere to be seen, but the nylon string, he noticed, was stretched tight and leading into the thick ivy and down the game trail.

I had to bend over real low to get down in there.

So, I went in to get the bucket, and I could see it sitting in the bushes on the right-hand side a short distance down the trail. The top of the bucket was laying over to the right. I got the bucket and saw that there was only a little bit of water and one minnow in there. I thought it was strange. I had bought three dozen minnows, and I didn't see any laying on the trail or the ground anywhere nearby. Then I noticed a track near the bucket. It looked just like a bare human footprint, around twelve inches long, and I first thought that it was mighty early in the season for someone to be walking around down here with no shoes on. Hardly anyone, outside of my family and a few childhood friends, even knew the trail existed. It was a mild day, with temps in the fifties, but still too cold to be walking around barefoot in the mud.

Crawling a bit further into the thicket, Darrell saw, about twenty feet away to his left, another minnow bucket and, about ten feet beyond that, the third. Happy that he'd found his missing bait buckets, he made his way back out of the vines. He would go on to tell me, I kept looking at that footprint. It dawned on me that maybe there were Bigfoot in the area with me. That maybe this was another one of those things and that I didn't want to be anywhere near another one. So, I got my things and left.

The whole series of events nagged at his pride for the next two weeks. Did he even want to go back there if the creatures were there? Was he going to be scared away from his fishing hole and never fish again? He'd already given up hunting because of them. After all, he'd already been three times, and they hadn't wanted to harm him. In fact, they hadn't even shown themselves, and he'd never felt scared or threatened in any way. Whatever it was seemed only interested in his bait, not him. He had never been a coward, and the notion of giving up his cherished fishing spot got the better of him, and he made up his mind that he was not going to give up. So that next weekend he went back, this time carrying his shotgun along with his fishing gear, just in case. He wasn't intending to shoot or harm anything, but he didn't want to be harmed either, so better safe than sorry, he thought.

He set his minnow bucket down in the same place as before, no strings attached this time, then went about casting his poles out into the river, no bait attached this time. This time, Darrell wasn't there to fish at all. He was there to watch and wait. He sat there on his upturned bucket, pretending to fish for several hours, paying close attention to his surroundings, especially the game trail to his left, before he saw anything move. Then, his patience was rewarded by the sight of a dark figure squatting down behind a tree about fifty or sixty feet down the trail. It leaned its head out and peeked at the faux fisherman, then darted back behind the tree, which was too small in diameter to conceal the lower portion of its body.

This one was smaller. Maybe about five feet tall. It

was black in color, but not as black as that first one I saw at my granddad's place. It looked more like the one in the Patterson-Gimlin film, Patty. It didn't look evil or demonic like that first one, and I felt no sense of fear this time.

The game of hide and peek went on for about two hours until it started to get dark, then Darrell decided to leave, but he returned the next day bearing gifts of food. He got as far down the game trail as he could go, wedged a board in the bough of a tree where he found more bare footprints in the mud, and placed several items of fruit on the makeshift shelf.

After I started gifting these creatures, I would go there as often as I possibly could. Sometimes every other day, sometimes every day. After a while, I learned what kind of food they liked and what they didn't. They wouldn't touch bananas for nothing, but they loved cantaloupes and donuts, especially the jelly donuts. They loved the blueberry jelly-filled donuts, but their favorite food of all was bacon. Cooked bacon. They wouldn't touch it raw.

Six months into his experiment, he got the idea to bring them a bag of toy whistles that he'd bought at the local dime store.

I bought a bag of those plastic toy whistles. There were eight or nine of them in the bag. You know, those small, cheap, plastic toy whistles with a string attached.

These were red, with red strings. I went back to the fishing spot and hung those little whistles up in the trees all around the area. It was a day or two later, on a Saturday when I went back and saw that all the whistles were gone. I always went in the mornings whenever I could, and I had started bringing a fold-up chair with me to sit on instead of a bucket. I was sitting in that chair, and I had my brother's pistol with me at that time. A .357 magnum. More for my own safety and peace of mind then with the intention to harm. After that first encounter at my grandfather's farm, I wasn't about to take any chances. I sat there in that chair for three or four hours that day, then I started hearing those whistles coming from the woods way on down the riverbank. That's when I knew they weren't just dumb animals. They were smart. Smart enough to figure out those whistles at least. It was kind of funny, really, sitting there and hearing them blow those whistles that I left for them.

Over the course of the next two years, as the creatures became more familiar with Darrell and his frequent visits, they began to get closer and closer to him. There were three different creatures in all that he was able to witness: a juvenile female, a juvenile male, and another male, a larger one, that stood six and a half to seven feet tall that always stood a few feet behind the young ones, obscuring itself by standing behind trees and brush. Darrell could hardly believe that these things, which he had always thought lived in the Pacific Northwest area of the country, could be so prevalent in the state of Tennessee. Yet here they were, eating his bacon and donuts and blowing his whistles. It was the darndest thing.

Eventually, the two juveniles became more comfortable showing themselves to the man, with the female being the more curious, or least shy, of the two. The closest she ever came to him was fifty feet away, Darrell said. The young male was always about five feet behind her. The taller male, which he thought wasn't fully grown, when he would see him, he would be about ten feet behind him, watching from the trees. He could now see the features of the young female, whom he described as being five feet tall, with black eyes, hair and skin, slightly long arms with a short, stocky body type. The hair covering her body was long and coarse, unlike the creature that he had first seen seven years previously, which was covered in what appeared to be fur, not hair. Her face looked like more of a mixture between ape and human than a devil, with a rounded, almost elongated head with no sagittal crest. Upon seeing the two, Darrell would always stand up and say, "Hello. How are you?" Then, he would tap his chest with one hand and say, "My name's Darrell. DARRELL." She offered no reaction at first, but after he had introduced himself like this for several weeks, the creature actually spoke back to him. In a low, guttural voice, she said, "UH-LEE-UAH-NUH."

Often, and much to our chagrin as investigators, we interview witnesses to creature activity who are completely honest and sincere and simply wish to tell the truth. But, sometimes, they don't tell the whole truth. Sometimes, they leave out certain details that they think would just be too hard for others to believe. Something they feel would make their story less credible. This is only human nature, after all, and no one is to blame, but still, it's important when trying to solve any mystery to have all the clues. Darrell has been interviewed several times, and he's always felt like he should withhold this information, which I present here for the first time. I want to congratulate Darrell, and all other witnesses like him, for finally coming forward here for this book and for sharing this information with everyone.

I could hardly believe my ears when she spoke. So, I looked at her and said, "Aleana?" and she just looked at me like, yes, that's my name. There, toward the end of that two-year period, she got to where she would even grunt 'Bye' when I left. I guess she was imitating me, because I would always tell them bye when I was leaving. They seemed like they wanted to be friends but were just as scared of me as I was of them and would only come so close to me and no closer"

It got to the point where the creatures were so comfortable with his presence that Darrell bought a cheap, disposable Kodak one-shot camera and took it with him on his next trip. Sure enough, and much to Darrell's delight, Aleana and her brother didn't seem to mind having their pictures taken at all, and he sat there and snapped away for several hours. Darrell dropped the pictures off at the local Walgreen's later that day to get the film developed expecting to have captured the best evidence for the existence of Bigfoot ever, but the next day when he picked up the envelopes containing the photos, he saw that every picture on the roll had turned out completely black. Upset, he demanded to know what had happened to his pictures, and after an examination of the negatives from the roll by the film developer, it was concluded that the camera that he had purchased had been defective.

Dejected, he left the store and didn't return to the river for two weeks. Then, armed with a couple more disposable cameras, he returned to try again.

When I got back there, I couldn't believe my eyes, Darrell said. Somebody, I don't know who—the city or the water treatment plant—somebody had taken bulldozers and excavators down there and completely leveled the whole area of all the vegetation and trees. All the vines, everything was gone and leveled flat. I just couldn't believe it. Why had they done that? Why right there at that spot? I was crushed. Afterwards, I went back down there back and forth looking for them for the next twenty years, and I never saw them again. I hiked back along that riverbank for miles and miles and even camped overnight hoping to find them. They were gone. Just gone.

Darrell claims that this experience helped him put to rest a lot of the fear that he'd been dealing with since his first encounter and that he now realized that there must be more than one type of Bigfoot and that the ones around his area of Ridgetop, Robertson County, were nonaggressive if not downright friendly. That helped put my mind at rest quite a bit, he said. I was more or less at peace after this regarding these things which we are told do not exist.

But that peace would later be shattered into a million pieces in a most alarming manner.

Third Encounter

After going through all of that at his fishing hole, as one might imagine, Darrell's interest in the Bigfoot phenomenon only intensified. He doubled his research efforts into the subject, and in 2000, he formed a small team to go out and actively investigate local Bigfoot sightings and activity, which they did for several years. In 2017 Darrell and his group were called to investigate a case down in Cheatham County, just thirty miles south of Darrell's farm in Ridgetop. The property in question was located along the Cumberland River and the scene of much previous creature activity. The owner of the house was a truck driver, a job that frequently kept him away from home overnight, and these creatures were said to be coming up and stealing vegetables from their garden and items from their deck, as well as looking in the windows of the house, which scared the man's girlfriend to death.

This truck driver had called my partner to see if we could do anything about it. So, we went down there and looked around and found a spot where we thought these things were coming onto the property from the woods. We found footprints in the area and other signs that they were coming through there. So ,we started gifting them just like I had done twenty years earlier, and just like before, bacon and cantaloupes seemed to be their favorite foods, which gave me a glimmer of hope that I might have finally found the ones that had been run out of my fishing area.

Darrell and his team ended up investigating the area for several weeks, during which time Darrell's partner, Billy Howell, was able to twice catch a fleeting glimpse of a massive, hair-covered creature that walked bipedally. Dave, the homeowner, also claimed to have witnessed the same creature, or a similar one, behind his garage one night. He also invited a well-known researcher, who had a fancy website and everything, over from Kentucky to share data. The researcher and his girlfriend ended up staying a couple of days there, and on the second night, they heard the sounds of something rummaging through the items at their campsite, but the researcher decided that he really didn't want to step outside the tent to see what was going on at all. After an anxious night, the researchers beat a hasty retreat.

We had set the gifting station up about two hundred yards out in the woods behind his garage, Darrell said. We would go there once or twice a week, mostly at night, and just sit, about fifty yards apart or so, to watch and listen. We heard those things breaking branches and cracking limbs in the woods many times, but we could never see them. I actually did end up seeing a female and a juvenile Bigfoot there before it was all over, but the thing that got me was—the more we went out there, the stranger things got.

During the last week of research at that location, Darrell and his fellow researcher, Mike, were set up in the woods about a hundred yards from the gifting spot. Darrell stationed himself at a tree, and his partner was sitting at another tree to his left, and it was getting late in the evening. In front of them was a dip in the terrain that went up into a small rise. Another hundred yards deeper into the woods beyond the rise, a light suddenly sprang from seemingly out of nowhere. According to Darrell, the object could best be described as a large, brightly glowing light bulb hanging three or four feet above the ground. It then descended to the ground and started walking toward the two astonished witnesses.

I watched this thing moving toward us for a good twenty minutes, It was moving slowly through the trees and brush. It looked just like an extremely bright light bulb, it was that bright, and it was coming straight toward me. When it got to the tree right next to me, I pulled out my gun and was ready to fire on it. I didn't know what it was. Mike had a really bright flashlight, and he shined the beam over on it, and—I know this is going to sound crazy. It is crazy—but right before both our eyes this bright light turned into an opossum. It went from a glowing light like a light bulb into an opossum! Well, of course we couldn't hardly believe what we were seeing. The opossum turned around and started walking back in the direction it had come from.

We were both surprised that we could see it so well in the dark as it walked back into the deep woods.

The two men sat in stunned silence for another thirty minutes, then two large, pulsating balls of light, about the size of beach balls, appeared in the forest in the same area from which the first light had come, and the opossum had gone. They began to travel through the forest, moving together, side by side along the forest floor. Then, the lights stopped. It's hard to describe what they looked like, Darrell told me. They had smaller lights inside them and were pulsating red, blue, and pink. They sat and watched the two stationary objects for twenty minutes, then both the lights rose upward and began moving forward, weaving in and out of the trees in unison just a few feet off the ground, traveling down the hill toward the gifting spot.

Deciding they had seen more than enough for one night, the two men got up and left the area at once. Once they had made it back to their truck, they started down the gravel road, which made a big loop around the area, and from the safety of the vehicle, they watched the lights as they moved all the way through the woods and disappeared out of sight. The whole experience "weirded them out," to use Darrell's words. We didn't know what we were getting into. We had never seen anything like that associated with Bigfoot activity before. We went back that next weekend and got into Mike's hunting blind, which was still in the same spot where he had seen the huge creature a few weeks earlier. It was about eleven-thirty at night when we got there and got situated. There was a swampy, wooded area to our left and, in front of it, a sage grass field about three hundred yards wide, bordered by more dense woods.

Not long after they arrived, they heard what sounded like a large pack of coyotes howling and barking from the wood line. Mike had a FLIR and, using this, they both got to see the pack as they ran through the sage grass quite swiftly, as if chasing something. Suddenly, the entire pack of canines became silent, and their heat signature no longer registered on the instrument. It was like they just disappeared. We couldn't see them on the FLIR anymore, and they completely quit barking, leaving us both in utter silence. It was eerie. Then from the swamp, we heard three loud tree knocks. Then, up on the hill to the right of us, we heard three more. Then, suddenly, there were these three tiny white balls flying in and out of the trees, traveling fast. They flew around us and in between some nearby trees, then went back into the woods and disappeared.

Darrell described the objects as about the size of golf balls, white and giving off no light at all. Immediately after this happened, both men started feeling sick. Darrell described a nauseous feeling. And I don't ever get sick to my stomach like that. Then a headache set in.

Suddenly, the car alarms of all three vehicles

that were parked two hundred yards away in the homeowner's driveway, including the homeowner's, went off all at once. Dave, the owner of the property, had been with them earlier but had since left to get back to his girlfriend. Mike's phone rang, and it was Dave's girlfriend sounding distressed and yelling for them to get back, that the creatures were in the yard, but they had already begun running when the alarms went off. They arrived to find the place in chaos, and after making sure Dave and his lady friend were okay, searched the area while the car alarms blared out insanely into the quiet Tennessee night. They found nothing. They did everything they could to get those alarms off, and nothing would work. It took them forever, he said.

After the harrowing encounter, Darrell just couldn't wrap his mind around all this weird stuff happening all at once and again felt "weirded out." He knew one thing for certain: he was ready to take a break from all this craziness—Bigfoot, orbs, morphing opossums, flying golf balls, all of it—and go back home and rest his mind. And that's just what he set out to do, but it seems the paranormal was not done with him yet.

That's when the weird stuff started happening at his home thirty miles away in Ridgetop. He was living by himself at that time. He and his wife had split up a year previously, and she had moved out with the kids to her own place in town. I started having problems at the house, Darrell continued. And I had never had any problems there before. I had a large farm. Large house. Couple of horses. A few days after we decided to leave the Cheatham case alone for a while, something started banging on the side of my house one night at about three o'clock in the morning. And I'm not talking about just banging on it a little bit. The whole house was shaking, and it was so loud. Whatever was out there was hitting the house so hard it sounded like it was trying to tear my house down.

Of course, he got up out of bed to have a look outside, walking around the entire perimeter of the house, but he didn't see a thing so, eventually, he got settled back down and back in bed, only to have the banging start again! Once again, he went out and searched, but saw nothing. The next night, the very same thing happened again, only on the other side of the house. The third night brought another round of heavy banging, this time from both sides at once! This went on for about a week, happening every morning from 3:00 to 4:30 a.m. Over and over again, he went outside carrying his shotgun, but could find nothing. Sleep was becoming hard to come by around the Denton homestead, not only for Darrell, as it turned out, but for his horses as well.

Darrell recounts: By the second week, it was still going on, and then I was woken up in the middle of the night by the sound of my horses going crazy out in the front field next to the stable. I got up, grabbed my shotgun, and went outside. Both the horses were huddled up all the way up next to my driveway at the gate. I couldn't get them to go back into the stables for anything. I went in there and turned the lights on. Had a look around but didn't see anything wrong, but the horses refused to go back in there or anywhere else in that field. They both just stood there next to the gate for three days, so I had to move them to another field.

One morning soon after, as Darrell was sitting on his front porch drinking coffee, he happened to notice that one of his sycamore trees in his front yard was damaged. Something had broken the top of the tree off about fifteen feet up and left it dangling down. That was odd, as there had been no storms or strong winds recently. He had planted that tree, and all the others, about six years before. It stood around twenty feet tall and was close to twelve inches in diameter. He walked down to inspect the damage and saw that the top had not been broken in two at all—but twisted—and there had been no storms in the area recently.

That's when he knew that the Bigfoot creatures had followed him to his home.

With all of this strangeness going on, I was at a point where I could no longer sleep at night. I had done my best to catch whatever was doing all these things, but I never did see anything. I had about twenty-five cats on the farm. You know the story. Momma cat kept having babies, and before you know it—most of them usually stayed in the barn or in the stable. Within a period of just a few days, every last one of them went missing. There wasn't a cat nowhere to be found. Not only that, but all the cat food disappeared too. The horses kept getting spooked, so I moved them out of that field into another field closest to the house. They still raised Cain at night, but not quite as much. I also had a herd of deer, mainly does and young fawns, that always slept in my front yard almost every night. I'd come home of a night and see them laying there. They disappeared next. All of them. I didn't see no more deer on that property until I sold it and moved out.

Darrell also mentioned that he'd had a wooden birdfeeder broken in two one night, and every morning, the gate to the outdoor pool would be standing open, even though it was a real pain in the ass to open. The latch would catch every time, and opening the gate was always a struggle for everyone who came over to swim.

Worried sick over the whole mess, Darrell called several friends who suggested that he rebuke these things in the Savior's name on all four corners of his property. He took their advice and rebuked these things saying, "I rebuke you in the name of Jesus Christ. Leave my property alone. You're not welcome here. Leave now in Jesus's name!"

After doing this, all the strangeness that was happening in and around my home stopped completely.

A mare had died shortly after this, and I had buried it out in one of the fields. A couple of days later I saw large, fresh, human-shaped footprints in the mud of the grave. Also, I would still hear the occasional tree knock or crashing sounds in the woods. So, I knew that these things were still active in the area, but they were no longer bothering my house and my animals. I truly believe that they followed me home.

So, Darrell did what any rational, sane individual would do in his shoes: he quit Bigfoot researching for good. I was done with it. I was no longer interested in going out into the woods and trying to encounter them. And feeding those things, I'll never do that again. I learned my lesson. It was so scary, you know, especially when my kids were in the house and all the banging was going on. That's not something that kids normally have to go through.

He later found out that someone had recently bought the adjoining property behind the Cheatham County research site, which butted up against the Game Reserve in Cheatham, Tennessee, and were in the process of building a house. The construction workers framed the house one day and had returned to the job the following morning only to witness in broad daylight large, man-like, hair-covered creatures dismantling the wooden framework and leaving it on the ground. They left the site and wouldn't come back; Darrell told me about the workers. They called the Cheatham County

Police as they were leaving. They had a news crew out there and everything.

Then things seemed to take a turn for the worse for Darrell. A thief had robbed him in a business deal and cost him everything. He had to sell all his homes, land, and cars just to make good on the money his partner had stolen from him. Creditors took just about everything he had and left him in a state of deep depression and despair. He even contemplated ending it all, but the love of his children made him realize how selfish that would be of him. As he stood inside the barn out back, gun in hand, his eight-year-old daughter walked in and said, "Daddy, will you come inside and eat a popsicle with me?" When he saw her little face, he burst into tears and dropped that gun, hugging her close and telling her that he loved her. And, like any real man would've done, he forgot all about such foolishness, took his daughter's hand, and walked back into the house to have that popsicle with her. In December of that year, he caught Covid, which nearly killed him, and he spent nine days in the local ICU unconscious and in critical condition with a temperature of 105 degrees. He believes only a blood transfusion, recommended by his sister, a nurse, saved his life.

After a couple of weeks of recovery, he went to the eye doctor for new glasses only to find that he was developing cataracts. Somehow, the doctor convinced him that he needed cataract surgery right away, which he then botched, leaving Darrell completely blind for nearly eight months. During that time, his experiences with the Bigfoot creatures plagued his thoughts. "Could they really be all bad? What about the ones down at the river? They were not mean or aggressive at all. In fact, they seemed to be curious at worst. The female, Aleana, might even be called downright friendly." Finally, as his eyesight slowly returned to normal, he made up his mind what he must do.

By September, his vision had returned, and just as he'd planned, he told his kids that he was going over to the Shenandoah National Park to camp for a couple of days. He loaded up some light gear and off he went. He had heard there had been some recent activity there, and he just had to know if all these things were evil or not. He had to find some closure, or it seemed that it would eventually drive him crazy. Later that morning he entered the park, found a place to park his truck, grabbed his backpack and sleeping bag, and disappeared up one of the many trails into the thick forest. Then he turned right and left the well-used trail behind him. For protection he had brought his pistol along packed safely away in his backpack—or so he thought.

He walked all day, he told me, seven or eight miles at least. Hours later, as darkness approached, he ran into a rocky bluff and decided to camp for the night. The next day, he planned to climb over the bluff and continue. He built a small fire and ate some of the meager provisions that he had brought, then unrolled his sleeping bag and settled in. The first night was peaceful, with nothing untoward happening. The next morning after coffee, he started looking around the area and was surprised to find footprints in some loose soil. On further inspection, he found what he believed to be a tree marker, a commonly reported aspect of areas with high Bigfoot activity. Excited at his discoveries, he decided to spend his remaining night where he was at. He was aware of the possible dangers involved in what he was doing. There was no cell phone service there, and he had only told his family that he was going off to camp for a couple of nights. The National Forest was a vast wilderness, and no one knew exactly where he was but himself, especially so far off the trail.

Night fell and he sat beside his campfire. There was a full moon hanging above him in the sky, but little of its light penetrated the thick blanket of greenery above his head. It started to get late, well after midnight, and just as he was thinking of turning in for the night, he started to hear movement in the underbrush to his left. He faced that direction then, with his back to the fire. At first, he could see nothing, but as the sounds came closer, he could make out the silhouettes of three large, bipedal creatures as they approached using the nearby trees for cover. But they may as well have saved themselves the trouble. They made an alarming racket walking through the woods, and the closer they got to my firelight, the more their eyes glowed yellow. I could see their eyes blinking, and I thought right then that I was just a fool. I reached into the pocket of my backpack where I thought I'd stowed my pistol away, but it wasn't there. I had accidentally left it in the glove compartment of the truck! I had a pin light with me that was pretty powerful, and I shined it over in that direction. I could plainly see them standing behind the trees because the trees weren't wide enough to hide them effectively. They would peek out at me, then dart back behind the tree.

Suddenly, without warning, four more yellow eyes appeared in the darkness to my right. Unlike the other three, they had approached soundlessly. They were all six to eight feet tall and covered with dark hair. I couldn't see anything but their outline and their eyes. I thought that this was it. That I was going to die by the hands of these things that weren't even supposed to exist. They were all spaced about twenty feet apart and, with my back to the bluff, I was surrounded.

Not knowing what else to do, Darrell attempted to strike up a rather nervous conversation with the creatures who, so far, had not uttered a sound, saying that he came in peace and wasn't here to hurt anyone or anything. He also asked if they knew Aleana, but the things just stood there glaring at him with their strange yellow eyes and not making a sound. Then, from the woods in front of him came more calamitous cracking of branches and trees. Something was walking through the woods toward him. Something huge. He could actually feel the ground shake with each footstep that hit the ground. A moment later and less than fifteen yards away, ten feet closer to him than all the others, a huge creature stepped into view, standing in front of two large trees, not trying to conceal itself at all. This one was a little lighter shade of "dark" than the other five, and it stood at least nine feet tall.

I was terrified, I started talking to it. I told it that I wasn't armed and meant no harm. That I was just using their forest, and I asked if it knew Aleana. It didn't respond, so I said, "Aleana! Aleana!" A second later, it let out these two low, guttural grunts, like it was answering me, but it was a frightful sound. There were six of these things all looking right at me, and I'm not ashamed to say that was the second scariest moment of my life, right behind my experience on my grandpa's farm.

Then, the big one turned and started walking nonchalantly back in the direction from which it had come. After it had left, the other five did the same thing. They walked quietly this time. Perfectly quietly. It was about 4:00 a.m. by then. I got my stuff together and headed back toward the trail as fast as I could. I was so glad to see daylight, and I eventually picked up the trail and made it back out of the park, all the while glancing behind me to see that the things weren't following me. I made it back to the truck around 12:00 p.m. that next morning

And that was enough for Darrell Denton. Questions answered. "Those things could've killed me, drug me off somewhere, and no one would ever even have known about it", he said. Darrell sold his house in 2022 and moved to Virginia. When he thinks about the events that he has witnessed and the strangeness that the Bigfoot phenomenon led him to, one more odd occurrence comes to his mind.

After that night in Cheatham County where the car alarms went off, we all went home, and Billy didn't have any problems. But that next day I noticed what I thought were two mosquito bites, one in the exact same place on both my forearms. These things wouldn't heal at all and were driving me crazy itching so much. Worse yet, I could feel a small, hard little knot directly beneath the bites. After suffering for about a week, I went to the doctor. He told me that they were insect bites, and they would eventually heal up. But they didn't. After another week of itching, I took a pocketknife to the one on my left arm. I was bleeding like crazy, but I finally managed to dig whatever it was out. It was about the size of a grain of rice, very hard and gray in color. I don't have any idea what it was, but I still have the other one in my right arm to this day.

1992 was a bad year for Darrell and another of his friends. A close friend named Martin Groves (see *Werewolves and the Dogman Phenomenon*), a well-known and well-respected deputy sheriff in Robertson County.

In 1992 Martin and a friend were turkey hunting in the Land Between the Lakes, on the Tennessee side, when they were harassed by what appeared to be a huge, hairy bipedal creature with a with the head of a wolf. They barely managed to escape to their truck, and when they started it up and the headlights came on, they saw two gigantic, hairy, evil-looking Bigfoot creatures standing there, almost as if the Dogmen (as there were more than one) were doing the bidding of the Sasquatch. As the two sped away, the evil Bigfoot gave him a thought that said, "We let you win. This time. Don't come back." Both the men suffered from health complications after the encounter. Martin's friend never recovered and ended up dying from one of those conditions. As of this writing, Martin is fighting brain cancer in the form of two malignant tumors.

In the entire history of the science of anthropology, there has never been any type of ape, of *any* genus, that has ever even been accused of having such abilities and keeping such sordid company as we have seen so far. That notion is patently ridiculous. But let's move on and try to answer the question that's been on your mind since the Bigfoot Michigan Rob story: Can seeing Bigfoot kill you?

5

Running in Place – Claudia's Story

"Everything I've ever done I've done out of a desire to help other people. Not to achieve fame or money, but to let people know the dangers that are out in there the woods."

Claudia Ackley was a kind, sweet woman who had dedicated nearly her entire life to helping others. She was also a gravely ill woman, but it wasn't always that way. Only after she became exposed to Inhumanoid monsters on multiple occasions over the last decade did her health begin to decline, which left her more than once lying at death's door. "It just seems like, when I have encounters or communications with these evil creatures, I get really sick. I've had three strokes already. I have a deadly blood disease which causes cardiopulmonary embolisms, or blood clots, to travel to my lungs. My heart is in such bad shape the doctors don't know what's wrong with it. My heart rate would speed up like I was getting ready to have another stroke, then drop down to twenty-one beats per minute. So they put in a pacemaker. Hypertension, hypoglycemia—the list goes on and on—but I was perfectly healthy until we saw the creatures in California. That's when I started getting really sick. I know it was the Sasquatch that did this to me," Claudia told me in an interview on Monday, June 26, 2023—an interview in which she agreed to share all her video and photographic evidence of the Inhumanoid creatures that were making her life a living hell after she'd moved to Bradley, Tennessee, three years previously.

Five days later, on Monday, June 30th, Claudia was found dead.

She had lived there in the Volunteer State with her

boyfriend in a lonely little cabin in the woods. Claudia told me that she'd had multiple encounters with both Bigfoot and Dogmen (as well as other things) there at the residence and had dozens of pictures and video evidence to prove it, including Ring Cam pictures and audio recordings, but that's not where her story began. It began in Ohio back in 2014.

We were living in Washington State at the time, in the city, she told me. And one day back in 2014, my youngest daughter approached me and said, "Mom, did you know that Bigfoots were real?" I was surprised that she said that. I'd never believed in any of that stuff. I was a city girl. So I said, "No, honey. It's called a myth. They're not real."

"How do you know?" her daughter asked. "Maybe

you should do some research."

And so, she did. This is the point her research into the subject began. Looking back on it now, I wish I'd never started, she later said. It was a huge mistake.

Every day while her two daughters were in school, she would research the subject on the internet and watch YouTube videos about Bigfoot. She soon became friends with many of the researchers and YouTube content creators that focused attention on the Bigfoot creatures. One of those friends invited her and her husband to a three-day camp-out deep in the woods of Washington State at a location of repeated creature activity. She attended, not believing at all that anyone would see Bigfoot, she told me, and resolved not to be overly disappointed if they didn't. She knew that she would not be impressed if shown any questionable evidence such as old, worn-out footprints and the like. She told me the first night there nothing at all happened. It was a perfectly normal, peaceful camp-out in the great outdoors. The second night they'd had rocks thrown at their group from the surrounding forest, which was a bit unnerving but not conclusive in any way.

On the third night, however, as the group was following a particular path through the woods, the YouTuber's dog, which they'd brought along, started acting strangely. I got the feeling that someone or something was watching me, Claudia said, so I looked to my right and saw what I took to be a juvenile Bigfoot clinging to a tree. It looked like a chimpanzee. He had huge, black, almond-shaped eyes that looked like an alien's, and he was up there holding onto a branch with one arm. As soon as he saw me, and knew that I saw him, he gave me a look of complete surprise and jumped down from the tree onto the ground. It took two quick steps on its back legs like a man, then dropped down to all fours like a monkey and ran off very quickly into the forest.

There were six other witnesses in all. All of them were stunned.

It looked like a flesh and blood animal. And after all her studies, that was her theory on the phenomenon from the outset, if they were real at all: that they were strictly physical creatures, an undiscovered species of animal.

When I saw it, I was completely taken aback that these things were actually real. That my young daughter had been right. Total surprise! But when I saw it, I was sure that my conclusions regarding the nature of these beings were correct.

Other members of the group who weren't in the immediate area saw it as it ran past them at an unusual rate of speed for running through the woods. So fast that it appeared little more than a blur to them. The experience began a fascination with the subject, which soon grew into an obsession so intense that her husband eventually told Claudia that it was either Bigfoot or him. She must choose one or the other.

After their divorce, her real journey began, a journey that she would never have chosen to take had she known the outcome of it all. As it stood, she was now free to continue her research, which she did with vigor, and soon met some famous people in the field. She was an amiable person and made friends easily wherever she went, having spent seventeen years of her life in the medical field caring for cancer patients. Over the next few months, and with the help of newfound friends, she was able to pursue her interest in locations all across the country in places like Oregon, Ohio, Washington, and Kentucky. I've been all over the United States, Claudia told me, and I never saw anything else other than footprints and alleged teepee structures.

But that was about to change.

Claudia and her daughters, at the time ages fourteen and eleven, ended up moving to California where they lived with her new boyfriend in a small, two-room cabin in the woods near the mountains. Claudia wanted her girls to know about and enjoy nature, so she was hesitant to speak to them about Bigfoot because she didn't want to discourage them from walking the numerous forest trails just outside their cabin door. She told me she felt safe there, but she was wrong.

One early evening in late March, after the girls had finished their homework and supper was over, Claudia asked the two if they wanted to go on a hike, to which they both agreed. She had just purchased an iPhone 5 for her oldest girl a couple of weeks earlier, and she was excited to do some snapchat videos in the scenic mountains. As they walked, Claudia gave her daughters some good advice concerning the animals that roamed the area. "If you see a bear, don't run," she told them. "Mountain lions are sneaky. Always be aware of what's above and behind you in the woods and never show fear to any animal."

But she could give them no advice about the "animal" they would ultimately encounter that day—an encounter that would change all their lives forever.

As they walked single file down the trail, they came upon the trees that had strangely all fallen over the hiking trail, and as her youngest daughter, who was in front of the line, walked around the third and last toppled tree, she saw two dark, hair-covered humanoid figures in the woods off to their right, standing on two feet. On seeing the girl's approach, the figures ran away into the brush. "The one in front looked really mean," her daughter later said. "I was really scared." The oldest girl and her mother didn't see the creatures. Claudia was snapping pictures at the time, but nothing could be seen in front of the group but her daughters. Her youngest stood there as if frozen, her hands down to her sides. Her sister then caught up to her and reacted the very same way to whatever the two were looking at. They just stood there, frozen in place.

I thought, "Oh, my heart," Claudia told me. There's a bear in front of them. So, I ran to them as fast as I could, taking the harness off the bear spray that I had brought along with us. When I reached them, I just couldn't believe what I was seeing. What she saw she later described as an enormous, dark-haired Bigfoot creature clinging to a large tree. The figure, she said, was covered in dark hair and was huge. She estimated that the thing was around fifteen feet tall and weighed around a thousand pounds. It had dark gray skin like rubber, according to her, as well as a pointed head, and black fingernails. The thing looked at the girls, then scratched its face with its black fingernails.

I didn't like the way it looked at my daughters, so I stepped in front of them, in between them and it. Then I heard a voice inside my head that said, "Don't come any closer." This was Claudia's first exposure to the way these things communicate telepathically, but it certainly wouldn't be her last. Stunned and not knowing what else to do, Claudia "whooped" at the creature twice. It then turned its gaze to her. The two girls were both terrified and wanted to go home. Still facing the massive creature, Claudia told them to calmly start walking back toward the car. She then turned and followed them, walking at a rapid pace until they reached the vehicle. Once inside, they quickly locked the doors, and the three sat in stunned silence for a moment.

It was like a horror movie, Claudia said. My oldest

daughter told me to put the key in the ignition and start the car. "Let's go, let's go", she yelled. I said, "Hold on a minute. What did we just see?" My youngest daughter, who was in the back seat crying, said, 'It was a man. A big, hairy Neanderthal man." None of the entities appeared to be aggressive in any way, and her daughter was able to capture images of the large one in the tree—twice!

That day, the children's innocence was taken away from them and carried into the dark forest. On arriving home, Claudia's boyfriend did not believe the trio of frightened girls until he viewed the footage. The next day, he and Claudia returned to the site where they found a human-shaped, five-toed print that measured twenty-two inches in length. He returned to their cabin convinced that they had seen a Sasquatch.

After that, I had to sleep with the girls, lights on, for a week. They wanted to move away from there immediately. My youngest said, "Mom, you lied. You told me monsters weren't real—and they are! Those things were not of God." Claudia, who was an atheist at that time, asked her why she said that, and the girl replied, "I saw their faces, Mom. They were demonic. They were not from God." Soon afterward Claudia called the DNR and was visited by a female agent who told her, despite her repeated protestations, that what they had seen was definitely a couple of wandering black bears. She admitted that some Boy Scouts in the area had recently been attacked by a bear and gravely injured.

Astonishingly, the agent didn't even bother to ask which trail they were on when it happened. Stung by the officer's refusal to do anything but provide a believable explanation for what they had seen and motivated by her lifelong passion to help people in need, Claudia made up her mind to do what no other person had ever tried to do: sue the state government for recognition of the hitherto unknown species in the name of public safety.

And that's just what she did. The paperwork was filed, and soon afterward, both she and her story became the subject of national news. A bevy of Bigfoot "heavy hitters" flew in to join in her lawsuit, help with her case, and/or provide expert testimony in court.

And that's when Claudia's real troubles began.

As she related to me during our interview shortly before her death, Claudia and her home soon became the focus of intense scrutiny by what she believed were government agents. Black vehicles would cruise by her wherever she went, as if they were keeping tabs on her whereabouts. Two men wearing black jackets walked up onto her porch one day and rang the doorbell. As she looked out the peephole, she inexplicably became frightened of them. Something told her from within not to open the door, so she didn't. Eventually they left, but she had the feeling that they didn't go too far. Maybe they never went too far.

In the months that followed, her lawsuit ground to

a halt. Her lawyer eventually put the case on hold, and so it remains to this day, over six years later. While her legal struggles in California were dying down, other negative factors were just getting started. Unexplainable things began to happen in and around her home. Strange lights started buzzing the little cabin, one of which she was able to film. Bizarre mists would form in the yard for a few seconds, then disappear. Poltergeist activity began soon after. Worse yet, one night as she and the girls were lying in bed, a tremendous banging began on the outside walls of the cabin that shook the whole house, and she knew right then that the Bigfoot creatures had followed her home.

I had heard people say that these things had followed them before, she told me, and I was always like, "What? Followed them where?" But now I knew what they meant. These things were now coming to my house every night, which was only about a half mile from the trail where we had initially seen them. I had trail cameras set out around my house for the longest time, but they always avoided those. The Ring Cam they didn't seem to mind, and they would walk around outside in the yard at night. I saw a lot of scary things.

Due to his job, her boyfriend would often be gone for days at a time, leaving the girls there alone to fend for themselves with no firearm with which to protect themselves and no vehicle to escape should the need arise. During this time, the terrifying high strangeness events would intensify, leaving the girls continually frightened. The creatures seemed to be emboldened when this happened and would often walk right up onto the porch and look through the peephole. These things didn't seem to recognize the Ring Cam as a camera, she said. They would walk around in the front and back yards like they didn't have a care, like they didn't know or didn't care that they were being filmed.

The girls were in a constant state of fear and begged her to move them out of the cabin and, as the funny lights lit up her yard and the creatures that couldn't exist looked into her windows and peepholes, it began to dawn on Claudia that she had been wrong about these things after all. Wrong about Bigfoot. Wrong about the reality of UFOs and orbs. Wrong about the existence of spirits. Wrong about all of it. These things were all related somehow, in some way that she didn't understand. But she soon would.

After a juvenile Bigfoot creature tried to break into one of the back windows one night, of which she was able to take a picture, she started calling 911 Emergency, but the local police turned out to be of little help. The thing was gone by the time they arrived, of course. Responding officers found multiple sets of prints of large, bare, human-type feet ranging in size from seventeen to twenty inches long in the deep winter snow around the cabin. Stranger still, at least one set of prints displayed only three toes. Despite the evidence to the contrary, the officers still insisted that it had been nothing but a large black bear attempting to get into the house to find food. It seemed that the official narrative regarding Claudia and her claims had been set, which enraged Claudia, but what could she do?

Her feelings of dread intensified in the following months. One night she looked up to see a tall figure watching them through the window—and it wasn't a Bigfoot. It was demonic, she told me. That's the only way to describe it. It was tall and skinny, with white skin and large black eyes. It looked so—completely evil. That's when I knew for certain that the Bigfoot phenomenon was so much more than what it had seemed to be in the beginning. I realized that all of these things had to be related and, if anything was related to that demon with dead, black eyes looking at us through the window, it had to be evil as well. She no longer believed that her children were safe and reluctantly agreed to let them both go stay with their dad, who lived in another part of the state, until things settled down. But they didn't. In the late winter of 2019, everything would take a major turn for the worse.

On Thanksgiving Day, November 25th of that year, Claudia found herself alone in the house. She'd managed to get herself a vehicle by then, so she didn't feel so trapped there, alone and helpless with all this insanity and no way out. But the car only served to provide a false sense of security that day, as it turned out. There was no escaping what was about to happen to her.

The girls were with their father, she said. My boyfriend was at work, and I was alone. We had to keep all of the windows covered because all of these things would come at night and look inside the house through our windows. On Thanksgiving Day, I looked out the curtains and saw numerous dark figures surrounding my house. It was them. The creatures were back and this time in broad daylight. I was too scared to leave the house.

For the next several hours, the creatures stood outside in the snow watching Claudia as she watched them from the windows of her house. There was three feet of snow on the ground that day, she told me, and they just stood there watching me. Weather doesn't affect them at all.

Finally, when she could take it no longer, she telephoned her brother, who knew the situation there, and told him that the things were outside and she had to leave. She was scared to death. Her car was about twenty steps from her door, but the snow was deep, and she knew that moving quickly through it would be difficult. Avoiding the Bigfoot creatures would be impossible. Her opportunity came when, right before her eyes as she watched, the Bigfoot creatures standing in her yard simply disappeared. Vanished right before her eyes. They didn't run away. They were there one second, and the next, I couldn't see them anymore.

Seizing the moment, she grabbed the snow shovel and went outside, shoveling just enough snow to get to the car and get in. She saw that the vehicle was surrounded by large footprints but, strangely, she saw none leading away from it. The coast still seemed clear, and she was relieved when the vehicle's engine finally roared to life. She threw it in reverse and gave it some gas, but the car didn't move an inch! After several failed attempts to move, the truth of the matter finally hit her, and her heart sank like a stone.

That's when it dawned on me that the creatures hadn't really left at all, she told me. I just couldn't see them. They were cloaking! And they were holding onto my car and not allowing me to back up. Oh my God, I was so scared. All I could think about was making it back into the house alive.

She shut off the engine, flung open the door and stepped out, and that's when the huge "alpha male" came walking up to her. She almost fainted when she looked at him, so frightening was he to behold. He was huge. Much bigger than the others, at least ten feet tall, and his hair wasn't black like theirs, but a light gray in color and thin around the face and shoulder areas, allowing her to see that his skin was black, as were his eyes. Also, unlike the others, this one had pointed ears and looked very, very angry, almost evil, and he was standing only five feet away. That's when I heard this metallic, mechanical-sounding voice in my head, Claudia told me. It said, "Hah! We like you!" It was completely unnatural sounding, neither human nor animal.

Overwhelmed with fear and the knowledge now that every single aspect of these creatures that she once ignored or even laughed at—cloaking, telepathy, all of it—was true after all, and not knowing what else to do as she slowly backed up toward the house, she answered the thing. Not with her voice, but her mind.

"I . . . like you, too. I . . . I love you. I'm not your enemy. I just want to help you. To protect you." The pointed-eared creature just stood there looking at her with its dead, black, soulless eyes.

"Don't you want everyone to know that you exist?"

What happened next is so alarming that I should let Claudia tell it in her own words.

When I asked that question, its eyes suddenly went from black to bright red, and its face took on a look that, well, it looked like a devil. It felt like I was trapped in some nightmare or something. It then screamed, "Nooooo!" without moving its lips, and it screamed it at me so forcefully and loudly that it almost knocked me down. I can't describe the terrible sound of his voice when he did that. I scrambled into the house as fast as I could, feeling nauseous and disoriented—in a state of shock, I guess—and stumbled into the kitchen and called 911. When I told the dispatch that intruders were on my property and I needed help, the woman simply said, "You call 911 too much. We're not coming back out there again. Besides, the roads are all covered in snow. It's too dangerous." Then she hung up. I just couldn't believe it.

I suddenly felt really sick then and started vomiting blood. I passed out then and lay there on the floor for four days, suffering, regaining consciousness just long enough to vomit again and pass back out. No one came to help me.

After an urgent call by Claudia's brother, paramedics found Claudia four days later lying in a pool of her own blood, barely clinging to life, and rushed her to the hospital where they found that she had suffered a 98 percent loss of blood. Her prognosis was grim after she slipped into a coma. She would then spend the next eight days in the intensive care unit fighting to survive. Much to the relief of her family and the entire Bigfoot community as well, she did.

When she was strong enough to be released from the hospital, she flat out refused to stay at the cabin for even one single night, returning only once in the company of several friends to get her personal necessities. Everything else was abandoned. Furniture, appliances, tools. Everything. She rented a hotel room in town and stayed there for a month recuperating from the psychic attack that nearly took her life. In February 2020, after she had regained most of her strength, she and her boyfriend fled California, traveling over 2,000 miles away to Bradley County, Tennessee, hoping to escape the Bigfoot world forever.

But that was not to be.

She felt safe again there at the new place, she went on to say. At least in the beginning. The days went by, and her strength began to return to her. Again, her new residence was a small cabin in an isolated, rural location.

Then, less than a month later in February, she started hearing whooping sounds coming from the woods.

I can't tell you how I felt right then. It was a terrible feeling to know that there was no escaping these things. That somehow, these creatures had followed me across the entire country. They're evil. They're demonic. That's the only answer that makes any sense. Not long after, as she knew they would, the creatures started showing themselves to her. They had traveled across a continent to find her, and worse still, they'd brought all their strange weirdo friends along with them, and even some new ones. As the alpha male had said, they "liked" her.

She'd had Ring Cams installed in this house as well and was able to view much of the activity through them. The Bigfoot creatures, much as before, prowled about the cabin wandering up onto the front and back porches, still seemingly oblivious to the security cameras installed in the doors and the video that was being taken of them. One juvenile who was hiding behind her shed one night came right out in front of her when she spoke to it in her mind saying, "You don't have to hide from me." She owned a FLIR camera and was able to spot one standing outside in the darkness using it as well. This became a nightly occurrence, just like back in Cali, and Claudia again began to sink into despair. But she had one hope that everything would be okay. After she was shown the true nature of the Sasquatch creatures back in Cali, her views on the reality of the spirit world completely reversed. Her views on good and evil reversed as well, and her disbelief in God and Satan was shattered into a million tiny little pieces. She had purchased a Bible then, read it, recognized the truth it contained, and given her life over to Jesus Christ. This was the only way that she endured the next several months of nightly visits by not only Bigfoot, but a variety of other Inhumanoids as well. Whether that had any bearing on why those things followed her, one can only guess.

One night, she observed what looked like a large dog lying on the ground about ten feet away from the front porch. It resembled a large German Shepherd lying on its belly, and that's what she thought it was. Someone's stray had wandered into the yard, which was unusual because they had no neighbors. She went about her business washing dishes in the kitchen sink, and the next thing she knew it had walked up to the house—on two legs—and started looking in the kitchen window.

It lifted its lips up and smiled at me. It looked completely like a wolf. It had large, long canines like dinosaur teeth. It scared me to death. I told it to leave, that I rebuke you in Jesus's name. Then it disappeared. It didn't walk away. It just vanished right before my eyes. Then I walked down my hallway and collapsed. I'd had a stroke.

Claudia was airlifted to a hospital in Georgia, where they administered blood thinners. She recovered in a few days and was sent back home. "I need to tell the public that these Bigfoot and Dogmen will follow you once contact has been initiated, and they're dangerous. The public needs to know. We all need to start praying, and the reason I'm coming out and telling people is that if something ever does happen to me, I want everyone to know that this is real. This is not fiction or something I'm making up. It's reality."

So, Dogman, which was another subject that she had at first dismissed as ridiculous and merely the subject of fanciful fiction, was real as well. On Thanksgiving Night in 2020, she awoke to find the creature rummaging about inside her home. It eventually exited the dwelling, much to her relief, by *walking right through the wall like a ghost,* offering no confrontation with Claudia and no harm to her. In fact, it acted like it didn't even know she was there, contenting itself with rummaging through some boxes in the living room before leaving the house.

Other entities made themselves at home there as well, including one that was much more frightening than the creatures she had witnessed thus far, even though it looked like a human. Like a dead human. It had looked into her kitchen window as well and scared the daylights out of her.

It was tall and skinny, Claudia described it to me. It looked like a skeleton with thin, whitish-gray skin stretched over its bones. It had sunken in, black eyes as well, and looked like a long-dead reanimated corpse. And it was wearing a black hat.

It was as if the situation in California was repeating itself in Tennessee and, once again, she began to avoid looking out the curtains or opening them even a little. And also, just as before, strange lights began to appear in the sky above the cabin and in the surrounding woods. One night, she awoke to see the entire back yard lit up like it was daylight.

Text from Claudia to my personal friend, Larry Fischer:

"There were so many lights out here last night and, of course I woke up because the dogs were barking. I left them inside. I was too scared to let them outside. I don't know what they would do, but it literally looked like my back yard was on fire, and there were orbs everywhere. One of them was a very bright blue."

I completely believed that these entities were demonic now, and that they fed on fear, so I tried my best not to show fear when they came around. Because I spoke out and went to the government, I feel like they're trying to get me. I'm being honest. I feel like they know that I'm trying to make the public aware of them, and they don't like that at all. They hate me. I'm not afraid for my life. I know that God is the strongest force in the universe now, not these things. I believe that He is 100 percent with me.

After the strange lights (including orbs of different sizes and colors) began their almost nightly activities, Claudia saw other strange figures in the woods by her house. She'd never told anyone else about all these things before, I'm almost sure, but even though I didn't know her personally and had never met her, she spoke to me the very first time as if we were lifelong friends and felt comfortable discussing with me some of the more bizarre aspects of her experiences with the Inhumanoids. She saw the typical alien Grays, as well as what appeared to be a female alien hybrid that looked nearly human except for her face, as she walked through the woods wearing a blue gown. "There was something about those blue gowns", she said. She also saw another large figure wandering about in the woods there one night. It looked human to her except for his unusually large size she described. It was bald, or nearly bald, and it had white skin and was also wearing a blue gown. The Bigfoot creature would often hide behind her shed and eventually became quite bold, even going so far as to approach her one night. Again, her boyfriend was prone to spending days absent from the home, leaving Claudia by herself to deal alone with whatever might happen.

And things continued to happen throughout the following months and with each new inexplicable experience, her health began to fall into decline once more. Now, just as before, poltergeist activity started to manifest inside her home. She often heard scratching on both the inside and outside walls. Objects began to be misplaced or went missing entirely, and something inside the house seemed to delight in repeatedly calling her name. She sometimes saw reflections in the shower curtain when she was in the bathroom. Scary reflections. She often had dreams of blood splattered all over her walls, she told me. She once had a group of Bigfoot researchers over to the cabin, and she had gone out to rebuke the creatures once again, when suddenly she felt like something was happening to her and found herself levitating several inches above the ground. For anyone who might not believe the truth of this story, this event was also captured by her surveillance system.

And then there were the Little People. Three times in her life she had seen them, she revealed to me. She had seen the first one in California, but thought it was a figment of her imagination, even though she had never been prone to such things. She described it as being around three feet tall or less, chubby with bloody red eyes and covered with dark black, curly hair. It was carrying some kind of stick, she said, and wearing dark black pants and shirt. It disappeared behind the TV when she saw it, but it was not there when she looked.

The next two times they visited her were both in Tennessee while she was lying in bed recovering after two consecutive strokes. They manifested themselves to her as reflections on her TV screen while the set was turned off. This one was also covered in hair, but of a blond color, and it always kept its head down and didn't face her and wore no clothes of any kind. She would look to where the reflection exposed its location in the room, but couldn't see it standing beside her bed. Yet, again, its reflection was still there when she looked once more.

The second time she saw it was much the same as the first, as a reflection on the television screen, only this time, it *did* look at her. It had a hairy, featureless face, she said, except for its eyes, which were also red. Its eyes were mesmerizing, and she had to force herself to look away from their reflection on the screen to look for it in the room. It wasn't there, she told me, but when she looked back at the screen, there it was, still standing beside her bed watching her with its bloody-looking eyes.

Then, a scenario played out in the reflection that, thank goodness, didn't happen in real life. The little blond creature jumped up onto her bed, wrapped its diminutive hands around her neck, and started to choke her violently. This all sounds like something from a scary horror movie, but I assure you all, these are the words that she said to me. No wonder the poor woman couldn't get well. She was being tormented to a degree that is nearly impossible to comprehend or understand.

When we last spoke, she told me that she'd already had three strokes, heart failure with pacemaker installed, and was suffering from hypertension and blood clots that were threatening to travel to her lungs and kill her, as well as a laundry list of other serious or potentially deadly health issues.

For the next three years, as her health declined, the activity on her property had ramped up considerably. There were orbs appearing inside and all around her home, as well as in the woods nearly every night. She believed that these things were actually entities in spirit form after she watched one land in the yard one night and actually turn into one of the Bigfoot creatures right before her astonished eyes. She also believed that there was some kind of portal out behind her shed due to the frequency of the creatures appearing from that area and the fact that an orb came rushing from behind it one night and chased her into the house. She could feel the presence of evil when these things were around, she said. When asked why she wouldn't drop the lawsuit, which had been stalled in court for several years when we spoke, she said: "Everything I'm doing and have done has been for the benefit of the public, not for me or my personal gain. I never wanted any money or fame or attention. I just wanted people to know that these things are real, and they're out there waiting and very dangerous. People *need* to know this. They need to be warned so they can be prepared if something like this happens. It's like a nightmare that you can't wake up from."

Only her faith in God kept her from sinking into the deepest depths of despair. Four days after our last interview, Claudia passed away, leaving her two daughters and the entire Bigfoot community to grieve for her loss and wonder what happened to her. Why had she died so young? The official cause of her untimely passing, it was said, was due to a heart attack, and didn't have anything to do with her experiences. The vast majority of people did not know about all she had been going through down in Tennessee. They didn't know that she had been tormented daily by evil, demonic monsters for the last three years. A few of her family and friends did know it, and they wonder still.

Text from Claudia to Larry Fischer:

"My entire life, my whole mission in life has been to help others. That's why I worked in the hospital for 17 years. I worked as a pharmacy technician for ten years and then transferred to the cancer center where I had the honor of helping many, many cancer patients. It was truly an honor for me to work with them, but it got to the point where I had seen too much stuff. Then I got pregnant, so I stayed home with my two daughters until they were around 12 years old. Maybe these creatures don't like me because of that and, also, I think they don't like me because I don't react to them like a normal human does. I don't get scared of ugly faces or anything. I've had my hair pulled, they have physically gotten me sick, but I continue to go on because I want that to be an influence for others. God is the one that helps me get through everything. I used to think that Sasquatch were apes that have not been found, but now I know that's not the case. They are very paranormal and they're also evil."

So, did these creatures have anything to do with Claudia's death? Most certainly. She went from a strong, healthy woman, who was used to hiking ten miles a day in rugged backcountry all across the USA looking for Bigfoot, to an invalid only a couple of years after she finally found it. At least she felt that way. It has been suggested that she was so sick there at the end that she was delusional, confused, and hallucinatory and so nothing she says about her three-year stay in Tennessee can be believed, but this is simply *not* true. She was talking to me, Barton Nunnelly, Larry Fischer, and several others, including her mother, right up until the very end, and not a single one of us felt as if she sounded anything but completely coherent and fully in charge of her mental faculties.

Also bear in mind that Claudia was able to capture either photographic or video evidence of nearly *every* encounter she claimed to have experienced, some of which are reproduced in this book, which is something that no other researcher has been able to do—from fifteen-foot-tall ape-men in trees to dead men looking

in her window to unexplained aerial phenomena—
and one thing is still certain: even in this modern age
of technological achievements, hallucinations don't
turn out in photographs, and you can't take pictures of
delusions.

Text to Larry Fischer:

"What I don't understand is why they haven't
killed me when they've had so many chances to. Maybe
they have and I just don't know it yet. Maybe that's why
I've been having strokes and my health is always bad.
Maybe that's how they're doing it, with infrasound or
whatever. I don't know. I do not fear them when I look at
them even though my heart is racing. I stay strong. I've
told the alpha male here that I am not about them. I am
a warrior for Jesus Christ, and I will never change. They
understand English perfectly. They also speak English."

For those of you who *truly* wish to preserve the
legacy of this remarkable person, please take what she
said about these creatures to my associates and me very
seriously.

It may just save your life.

6

Hanging Tough – Jerimiah's Story

Jerimiah Fountain is one of the most down-to-earth people you could ever hope to meet, despite being built like the Terminator. Fountain, age forty-four, lives in the rugged timber country of the Adirondack mountains in upstate New York. He's a kindergarten teacher in a town called Constable in Franklin County, something one would never guess to look at him. He's the rugged, lifelong outdoorsman type of man, yet charmingly soft-spoken and humble. And honest. His family, all loggers by trade, had always lived there in the mountains. After high school he went to work with his family, felling mighty trees, stripping them of limbs using a huge machine called a skidder, then loading them up on the back of semitrucks and shipping them off to the lumber company for processing. He left the family business when he decided to pursue his lifelong interest in mixed martial arts. This opened up a whole new world for him, and he spent the next fifteen years traveling the world and doing something he loved to do: full-contact competitive fighting.

A traumatic brain injury, or TBI as they are called in the medical field, ended all of that, and after moving to North Carolina for a couple of years, Jerimiah and his wife returned to his family's 250-acre farm in New York in the fall of 2021. Jerimiah had heard about Bigfoot before. His grandpa used to tell him stories when he was a kid. Stories of hairy boogers that lived in the woods. Not to frighten him, he knew. Grandpa wasn't about any bull, but straightforward, honest, and to the point. His grandma was a full-blooded Mohawk, and she told her stories as well: stories of the *Ot-ne-yar-hed*, or Stone Giants as her people called them in the old days. Loggers would often see these creatures while plying their trade in the Adirondacks. There's one story of how a team of loggers were stalked for several days while clearing some timber back in the 1930s. When the mountain devils finally showed themselves at less than fifty feet away, the team left in a hurry, abandoning the site, their tools, and their pay, and never came back. Listening to all these tales passed down from his grandparents made a big impression on the young Jerimiah, and he developed a keen interest in the subject. It was an interest that would never leave him and was rekindled with earnest upon his return to the mountains.

In an interview in 2023, he told me he had seen these Stone Giants himself on three different occasions.

The first time had been in the late fall of 2001 while hunting on his family's land. It was late in the afternoon, and dusk was threatening to catch him before he could reach his truck, which was parked about a mile away. It was muzzle-loader season, and he was carrying his gun and a backpack with him. It had been an unsuccessful day, and he was tired and a bit annoyed with himself for staying too late. He was still about a quarter of a mile away from his truck when darkness made good on its threat. There was some equipment and a skidder sitting on the side of the road, left there from a recent job, and as Jerimiah approached it, he saw a pair of glowing amber eyes at the front end of the skidder. As he came closer, he noticed that the eyes would disappear from the front of the skidder, then reappear at the back. This happened several times, as if whatever it was were peeking at him and trying to avoid being seen. Now it was at the front again, and he could see the shape of a rounded head and broad shoulders that had a humanlike shape. As he got closer, whatever it had seemed to give up on the idea of not being seen, and it wrapped its left arm around the front end of the logging machine.

I stopped in front of the skidder and hit it with my headlamp. There were two large logs lying twenty feet apart and about fifteen feet in front of the skidder. I could see this thing's eyes shining really bright now. I was kind of freaked out by the fact that I could see its eyes shining even before I turned my headlamp on and also when I turned it off. Suddenly this thing leaps out from behind the skidder so incredibly fast—it was just unbelievable.

Astonished at what he was seeing, he could do nothing but look on in disbelief. There was something odd about the way it moved. Something that he'd never seen any animal do before.

When it jumped, there was no bend to its knees at all. Almost like it was hopping, using only its toes to push off and up. There was no other movement of the arms or legs at all. This made it look almost like it was gliding. It jumped to the first log, then off to the second one, and then it leaped or glided back behind a tree about fifty feet away from me. I was astonished, and I remembered what my grandma had always told me about the nature of these things. She said that they were creatures with feet in both worlds, meaning the physical world and the spiritual one.

Jerimiah described the thing as being about five feet tall, weighing about two hundred pounds, and solidly built. It was covered in brown or auburn-colored hair that looked to him to be extremely clean and well-groomed, like it had been freshly brushed. Its head was shaped like a blend of human and ape, with no sagittal crest. It had long arms and was quite athletic-looking and muscular. It was too dark to notice if it had either female or male genitals, he said.

The thing stepped out from the tree a bit and

into the light of Jerimiah's head lamp, where it stood watching him with those strange eyes and bobbing back-and-forth motion. I honestly thought that an orangutan had escaped someone's private zoo or something and was running around on my dad's farm, he said, which was passing strange since we didn't have any other neighbors near our property. Not knowing if his life was in danger or not, and unable to think of anything else to do, Jerimiah raised his rifle and pointed it at the creature. When he did that, the thing raised up its right arm, put his hand over its face, ducked back behind the tree, then took off. He figured that would be a good time to get the hell out of there. And that's exactly what he did.

Jerimiah's second brush with the unknown came in 2007. That first experience had soured him on the pastime of hunting, just as it did Darrell Denton, for a long time. He no longer relished the sport as he used to, especially the part where you're all alone in the woods not really knowing what else was out there with you, just waiting in the darkened forest. Now that he knew the Stone Giants were an actual part of reality and not some tribal myth, everything had changed for him. But, after completely staying out of the woods for over two years, only going back in for short intervals or on work errands, he had finally got up enough resolve to try hunting again. Time has a way of dulling our better judgment sometimes, and it would only be a matter of time before he would regret his decision.

Again, it was late fall, hunting season, and Jerimiah had gone out to work on his tree stand. He was carrying a .300 Magnum pistol and no rifle, as he had not planned on hunting that day, just getting his stand ready to use. It was around 3:00 p.m. About an hour later, when his work was finished, he thought, "What the heck? I might as well climb up in the stand for a while before heading out." As he sat in the stand, he heard what he described as a "loud moaning, howling, yowling scream." He'd never heard any sound like that before coming from any animal, and he was familiar with the animals of the area. He thought it best to leave immediately.

There was an artesian well just down the road from his stand, which was where the sound had come from, and he had to walk right by it to get back to his vehicle. He got down from his stand and started walking. As he approached the well, he noticed what he thought to be a tree standing in the pond. Strangely, he'd walked by that well many times and had never seen it before. The tree was standing with one moss-hung branch held high. He eyed it as he continued walking toward it, not realizing what was going on. When he got to within forty feet, the "tree" turned its face and looked at him. Now he could see clearly what it was; an eight-foot-tall, seven-hundred-pound Bigfoot covered in long, brown hair. He could see by the creature's furry breasts that it was female. It stared at him with large black eyes that made his heart skip a beat.

"It was absolutely massive," he told friend and colleague, Barton Nunnelly. It wasn't muscular like the first one I saw, but built very solidly, stocky looking. I couldn't believe how big it was. It was three feet thick from front to back, but what really impressed me most was how huge and strong the hips and buttocks of this thing were. It had a large head, with no hair around the face and mouth areas, a flat nose, and the mouth was so wide, almost from ear to ear, that it reminded me of a Pez Dispenser. It looked like she could bite my head clean off if she wanted to.

Bizarrely, Jerimiah claims that at the bottom of each of this thing's black eyes was a nictitating membrane, like a lizard or a crocodile, that was lighter in color. This membrane flickered at the bottom several times, as if the creature was trying to decide whether to use them. Since it wasn't quite dark at the time, Jerimiah is absolutely sure of what he saw.

Jerimiah instantly drew his pistol, of course, and then the thing looked at him and he knew, somehow, exactly what that look meant: Pull that trigger, and you're dead. Don't pull it, and you can live. Jerimiah chose to live. That pistol would've only made her mad, he said. I don't think it would have been capable of killing or even wounding her too badly. She took one hop out of the water and onto the bank. This was about a ten- to twelve-foot leap, and she was standing in three to four feet of water at the time. Then she jumped three more times into the forest and was gone in an instant.

The thing didn't run away at all, he assured Barton, but leaped away in the same effortless, gliding manner as the one he saw six years previously.

The next day, he returned to the spot to look for evidence. Strangely, this thing left no tracks, he said, only scuff marks on the ground where it had landed after jumping. They measured the distance between the three leaps that it performed the previous evening at a total of sixty-three feet, or twenty-one feet per leap.

Jerimiah started getting into the subject a bit more after that, spending much of his free time reading and researching Bigfoot, but it wouldn't be until twelve years later that he would see the creatures again and, as you might expect at this point, they didn't come alone.

In May 2019, Jerimiah and his family were living in North Carolina and had picked out a local spot in Vanceboro to focus their research efforts upon. They made frequent visits there, usually at night. The area was known in Bigfoot circles as a regular hotspot for the creatures. It was a lonely, wooded spot near some train tracks with a trestle that ran across a large creek. The trestle was about fifteen feet above the water there. The whole family had taken an interest, to one degree or another, in Jerimiah's passion for cryptid research. His wife, Stacey, his then fifteen-year-old daughter, Xzandria, and his twelve-year-old son, Xzavier, were all out with him that night when Xzavier spotted a tall figure as it ran across the railroad tracks and into the forest.

They would often hear footsteps walking through the water, as well as vocalizations and other things said to be associated with Bigfoot. Once, the thing left a handprint on one of the pillars that supported the trestle, which Jerimiah was able to photograph from a boat. Then, bizarrely, or completely predictably depending on your point of view, they started seeing lights in the sky and our old friends, the orbs, made their appearance as well. The small balls of colorful lights would often follow them as they walked through the woods beside the creek and even allow them to make videos of the experiences. One night, Xzandria and her mother, Stacey, heard the sounds of multiple large figures walking through the creek and soon after observed both red and blue eyeshine approaching them. His daughter yelled, "Oh my God, Dad! What is that?" Jerimiah quickly lit up the targets with a spotlight, but only one figure could be seen walking along the edge of the creek about sixty feet away.

This one was different, Jerimiah said. It was light gray in color, almost silver, and its eyes shone a fluorescent blue. It had a completely round head with a very gorilla-like face.

Judging by the brush it was walking through with

seemingly no effort at all, Jerimiah guessed its height to be around eight feet tall. The family watched as it drew nearer to the opposite bank. It looked at them once with eyes shining like car headlights, then stepped out of the creek, walked up the hill, and crossed the tracks. They could all see its eyeshine as it walked up the hill, even when it was turned away from them, and they all could hear it as it walked away.

Two nights later Jerimiah and Stacey returned to the location, but this time they chose a vantage point on top of the train trestle looking down into the creek fifteen feet below. They didn't have to wait long before they heard the sounds of something big and heavy walking through the water below and coming in their direction. Then a white orb appeared as it bobbed up and down over the water, slowly following the sound of the footsteps. But the two intrepid investigators were ready. Jerimiah immediately started recording video, and Stacey started snapping still photos in rapid succession with her phone. The sounds of heavy footfalls in the water approached the trestle directly below them, and then passed under them and out the other side, but they couldn't see anything. By now several more softball-sized white lights had drifted in from the same direction and joined the party. The footsteps faded off into the distance, and that's when they decided it was time to leave.

When they got home and reviewed their evidence,

they couldn't believe their eyes. The creature that had walked below the train bridge completely unseen by the naked eye was right there. The camera had picked up what the naked eye could not. The invisible creature was right there in both the video and the pictures!

And, as you may have guessed: it was no Bigfoot.

What the thing in the video looked like was more reptilian than anything else. It was tall and slender with gray-colored skin, a triangular-shaped head, and a pointed nose. Oddly, the figure looked to be carrying in its arms the carcass of a full-grown boar. The two could come to no other conclusion than the creature had been cloaked as it walked beneath them.

Friends, I hope you can appreciate what's being revealed to you here. This is the truth about this phenomenon. After moving back to New York in 2021. Both Jerimiah and Stacey, when asked, admitted they had experienced episodes of missing time while researching the Bigfoot hotspot in North Carolina on three different occasions. "We would walk in sometimes at 1:00 p.m., and the next thing we knew we were walking back out at 4:00 p.m."

More Inhumanoids were waiting for Jerimiah and family once they returned to New York. In 2016 Jerimiah and Stacey saw something dash across the road less than sixty feet away from them. It was brown in color, stood an estimated seven and a half feet tall, and had the head of a wolf. Its body resembled more of a Bigfoot as it did not have digitigrade, or lupine, legs. This was a Dogman, Jerimiah realized, which catapulted him into a whole other realm of Bigfoot Research, one that he was completely unprepared to consider at the time.

In the winter of 2021, a nine-foot-tall, black Sasquatch was seen looking into one of the back windows by a family member. All this caused quite a stir at the time.

In the spring of 2022, while out scouting for a good spot to turkey hunt, Jerimiah saw another strange "animal" standing in the brush about eighty feet away. It was tall and covered in gray fur and also had what appeared to be the head of a wolf. This one also had its arms wrapped around a dead animal, though he couldn't quite tell what kind it was.

UFOs were a common occurrence at their homes in both New York and North Carolina, Jerimiah said. Wherever there was Bigfoot activity, ninety-five percent of the time strange lights would appear in the sky, from small round dots to large triangular-shaped craft. His last Unidentified Aerial Phenomenon sighting, a blue orb, happened on July 6th, 2023, which proves that the area is still as active today as it's always been since the first settlers moved north and began cutting down trees.

And so it remains today.

7

Dying to Know – Marc's Story

The following was taken from my good friend and colleague, Sybilla Irwin's YouTube Channel, *Sketching Encounters*, and is used with her permission. It concerns a man named Mark from central British Columbia. His story is one that should be heard, so I present it to you now for consideration. Mark had a series of really intense encounters with these creatures, encounters that changed his life forever, and has been trying to cope with the effects of his experiences for over forty years now. Like the other accounts in this work, these weren't your ordinary garden variety relic hominids, or undiscovered apes, but something else. Mark had asked Sybilla, who is quite a talented artist, to render a sketch of one of the creatures he witnessed and, also, to allow him to tell his story because he felt that it was important and that people should know the truth, and the only way to do that is to step forward and share with others. At the time of his first experience back in the 1970s, Mark lived in a small cabin in the woods in the Cariboo region of British Columbia, and he had never even heard of Bigfoot.

The funny thing is I had no idea that his experience was so unusual. Obviously, it was very, very strange but, in hindsight, listening to other people's experiences and such, it really does kind of stand out.

This happened in the early to mid-seventies, he told me. I'd never even heard the word *Sasquatch* at that point. I'd never seen the Gimlin film. It was a total surprise. So these things all came slowly. I was about twenty years old, and I had moved up into this little cabin to spend a year or two in the wild. I was running away from the city, I guess. I was born and raised in Vancouver, and I wanted to get out into the country and spend some time in the wilderness. To just experience that. I had an opportunity to work on this cabin that my family owned. I was happy to get up there. I just loved it. I went up there with all my food and everything that I thought that I needed to live up there. Fishing equipment. I had an old .30-30 rifle, which I never used, but I figured I was pretty well prepared.

So I got up to the cabin and everything was going well. It was so peaceful and so quiet. I guess the first thing that was unusual that started to happen were the wood knocks. Usually in the early evening I would hear wood knocking, and I thought it was somebody chopping firewood up on the hill, which was weird because there was no road up there, and nobody would be using an axe to cut down trees. I would hear them one night, and then another night, and another, and they sounded like they were getting closer. I thought that I would see him pretty soon, as it now sounded like he was chopping wood right next door. Then I realized that I couldn't be right. That wasn't what was happening. So, I just wrote it off. A lot of the things that were happening I didn't know what they were, so I had a lot to learn about the country and the wilderness. I just let them go over my head, you know? I didn't really think too much about it.

Stick snapping was another one. A big one, and it continued the whole summer. Sometimes right beside me, a very loud stick snap would happen. It sounded like a moose would step on a branch and snap it. Right beside me sometimes, and I would look, but I never saw a moose or a deer or anything. I didn't know what that was. It happened so often, in the daytime, too, not just at night but in daytime. And rocks—one morning I was eating my breakfast, and I heard this big splash, and I thought, 'Oh, that must've been a giant fish jumping in the water.' But I would see fish jumping out of the water all the time and they never sounded like that. It was a big rock about the size of a cantaloupe landing in the water and going SPALOOSH! And that would happen every few days, always while I was eating. And I never saw the rock. And I thought, 'Okay. Somebody's doing this.' And I would run down to the water and look, and there would be nobody there.

It was very remote. No neighbors in the area, just a few summer cabins, but at that time there was just nobody up there except me. These things kept happening, and I just shook my head and thought, 'Well, that's just the way it is out here, I guess. Sticks just snap sometimes by themselves.' And the rocks, I didn't have any idea what that was. Maybe big birds or something landing on the water. Of course, it wasn't that.

And then some of the stuff was a little more obvious. When I was working on the cabin and fixing it up, cleaning the yard and stuff, one time I'd raked all the rocks down smooth where I parked my truck because the area was quite lumpy. I was happy with that, but the next day I went out, got in my truck and started backing up, and my truck was bouncing all over the place. So I get out and look and there's all these rocks that I had cleared the day before, all placed underneath my tires where I would drive over them. They had placed them there. I thought, "What the heck?" I thought someone was playing a joke on me. It was kind of funny, and I think these things do have a sense of humor much like a person.

And then one day, after I had been there for a little over a week—and I think this is what really got the interactions started, it was almost by accident—I had went fishing and did really good. I'd caught four good-sized rainbow trout. I brought them back and cut all the heads and tails off and cleaned them, and I went to

throw the guts and heads in the water to let the birds
come and get them. They usually did that. This time I
got this feeling like, "Stop, don't do that!" And I thought
about it for a second and got the notion that if I did that,
it would bring in the bears or something. So I decided
to dig a hole and bury the guts and get rid of them that
way. It was a really weird idea, actually, now that I think
back, but I did that and thought it was okay. Then, for
the next few days, I'd walk by the spot where I buried
the heads thinking to myself what a dumb idea it was.
They were just going to rot and start to stink. Sooner
or later a bear's going to come along and smell it and
dig it up. And sure enough, I walked by and the dirt
had been disturbed and patted back down. So I went
and dug it up again. All the bones and guts were gone,
but the dirt had been replaced and it was patted down
again. I thought that was really weird. I had seen dogs
bury bones and such and scrape the dirt back over it and
pat it down with their noses, so I thought, okay, bears
must do that too. My head was telling me, "Bear, bear,
bear. Lookout for the bears," but the whole time I was
up there, I never saw a single bear or even any sign of
one.

So when I fried the fish, I took the frying pan—
it was an old cast iron pan—and put it in the lake to
soak it. I went back the next day to get it and clean it
up, but the frying pan wasn't in the water. I eventually
found it about a week later thrown over into the brush.
I could tell that it had been scrubbed or licked clean.

That happened a couple of times. One thing I fried bacon and the next day the pan was spotless. I mean licked spotless. And, after that, I remember the top of the fireplace. It had steel legs on it that were hammered into the ground. I came home and it was pulled out of the ground, which must have taken a lot of strength. I thought, "Oh, somebody doesn't like my frying pan and they don't like my stove either. Crazy."

Other things—the chairs. I would come home and all of my metal chairs in the yard would be pushed over. Never any of the wooden chairs, just the metal ones. This would happen every time, and I came to expect it. It was never any surprise for me to come home and see that. I've heard about gifting and such. How some people give them food, and I guess that's what happened. Accidentally in my case. I had no idea. I was so unaware of what was really going on. It wasn't until I actually saw them right in front of me that I knew what was going on.

One day I went for a walk, and I was looking at the ground for animal prints or sign, and I came across a dead grouse that something had killed and ripped all up. I thought that a coyote or fox had killed it. There were feathers everywhere and it had been eaten. There were the feet, a wing and a couple of other pieces left over, and it was all scattered around. A day later I went for a similar walk and came across the feathers again, but they weren't scattered. They were put in a neat little pile. I thought about that puzzle for a while. These Sasquatch, they're watching all the time, you know. They don't miss a trick, and they like their feathers. I came home from my walk and there was a little ball of feathers, wadded up and stuck together, laying in front of my door in a little ball. There were three different kinds of feathers in there: grouse, duck, and blue jay. That was another puzzle for me. How do three different types of bird feathers somehow work themselves into the same ball? Coincidence. Everything was a coincidence for me then. Later, I went to go in the back door of the cabin and there was another blue jay feather stuck in the crack of the door and sticking out like someone would leave a business card. I thought it must have been the wind. I had no other explanation. I brought it inside.

I had my head in the sand. I was so enjoying the work and the food and the life. I wasn't ready to start thinking about anything negative. So the gifting continued over the course of that summer. One day I came home and there was a crushed frog on my deck. It was still alive. I got in the truck one day and there was a turtle shell sitting in the middle of my seat—inside the truck. One day I picked up a dead dragonfly, and it was a great big one and a pretty blue color, and I looked at it for a minute to appreciate it. Then, when I went back home, there was another dead dragonfly placed in front of my door right where those feathers were. It was about three or four days later, and I had gone out. When I got back and went inside, there was the most beautiful dead dragonfly placed in my windowsill, in perfect condition.

Then things ramped up a little bit. I don't know. Maybe they were kind of getting used to me. But they got more pushy, too. The side of my cabin that was closest to the trees, it was like they didn't want me on that side of the cabin. I could almost feel it. I would take a step to go that way and I would feel the strong urge to go back. Step back. It was just sort of a strong feeling, and I didn't make much of it. I just found myself avoiding that side of the cabin.

One time my mom came to visit and asked me what I was doing with all that junk under the cabin. I didn't know what she was talking about, so I went and looked and there was insulation, boxes, and assorted other junk that had been pushed up underneath the cabin. I went to pull some of it out and I didn't know where it had come from. Never seen it before. So, I pull this stuff out, the further I go underneath the cabin, and here's this big area, ten feet around that looked like it had been raked to perfection. It was spotless and flat. I went to stick my hand in the soft dirt just to see how fresh it was, and I immediately got this strong thought in my mind saying, "No! Don't touch that!" And I recoiled back and then thought, "That's dumb. Of course, I'm going to touch that dirt." And I went to touch it again, and I just got the strongest feeling to get the hell out of there. Don't touch it. Back off. It felt like intense claustrophobia, and I just backed out of there in a hurry. I tried later to go back and finish cleaning it up, but I couldn't go in there. That feeling of claustrophobia would hit me again, and I just couldn't do it. So I decided to hide the garbage and junk instead. I couldn't bring myself to go back under there again.

There was this squirrel that used to come down on the tree next to the cabin every day, chattering and making little scratching noises with its fingernails as it climbed down the tree, and I would go out and feed it bits of food. I got used to that squirrel, and every time I'd hear it chatter and its nails clicking down the tree, I would go look for him. This happened nearly every day, and I got used to him being around, thinking it was really nice to live in a place so quiet that I could hear the wildlife so well. After a while, I started hearing the sound of his claws coming down the tree, but no chatter, so I looked out and I couldn't see my little friend at all, just hear the sound of him running down the tree. This happened repeatedly and I never could quite figure that one out. There was a grouse that would alight on top of an old tree stump and flap its wings, making a thumping sound. After I watched him do this several times, I would walk out and hear the sound coming from the tree stump but never see the grouse, or I would hear the thumping from inside the cabin and walk out to look at him but couldn't see him.

The biggest one was the loon. There was a loon that

lived on the other side of the lake and when I heard that loon, I thought, 'What a beautiful sound. So loud and clear and beautiful.' So I would go listen and I really loved the sound he made. I could see him there on the other side, and I just loved to sit and listen to him. Then I would hear the sound from inside the cabin and go out to look at him, but I couldn't see him. So I talked to a lady, a birdwatcher, and I was telling her about the loon and she said, "Yes, I hear them too and it's so unusual because loons migrate way early and there shouldn't be any around here right now."

I was finally starting to wise up. The stick snapping continued the whole time I stayed there. I remember one time coming home and not hearing anything for a couple of days and wondering what had happened to the stick snapper. Then, I was walking up to the cabin and something started throwing pinecones at me. Four little pinecones hit me before I made it to the door. I ran down the driveway expecting to see some kids with slingshots, but no one was there. And this was in the daytime. I had made a friend while I was there. He was nineteen, and I was twenty, and he would drive out from time to time to visit me and talk. I was glad for the company, as I hardly ever saw anyone out there. One night he came over and brought some beer and sandwiches and two girls with him. I thought, "Oh yeah! Beer and girls! Thanks, buddy!" But it didn't last long. We were outside, and I had just popped the top of my first beer when one of the girls jumps up and says,

"What was that?" She had heard something stomping out in the brush. I tried to calm her, but it happened again, and we all heard it. Then, a stick snap, the ones that I'd gotten so used to, sounded off right beside her. There was nothing there, but it was loud, and I tried to explain to her that sticks snapped all the time in the woods, it was a natural thing, but it scared the girls so badly, one grabbed the food, the other grabbed the beer, and they were gone! That was the lead up to the main event. The visitation that ended it all, including my stay at that cabin.

I had moved my cot in front of the big picture window up front. It was really pretty there when the moon was out and reflecting off the lake just a few yards away. I loved to go to sleep to that view. So one night, I'm lying there asleep in my cot, and two Sasquatch decide to come visit me. I could hear them coming. Hear their footsteps crunching in the gravel in the driveway outside. They walked very slowly. I'd hear just a single crunch and then nothing. Then another crunch and then nothing. Then a small twig snap, then nothing. I didn't care, really. I thought that if something was out there, it would go away. I'm tired and I'm not going to get up. Just when I'm thinking that I'm not getting up, I hear the voices. There were two. One was really deep. It said something, like some words or something, but they weren't in English. Then he got answered by another voice. This one was really different. It made buzzing and popping noises. They were going back and forth, speaking in sentences like a language. I raised up thinking, "Son of a bitch! I've got company!"

So, I looked out the window and didn't see anything out there and thought, "I must be really tired." And looked, and I didn't see anything at all. I could still hear them very clearly, though. And I got totally freaked out by this. I was thinking it must have been a dream or something. Then I hear the sound of creaking boards, like something really heavy is on them. Creaking as they bend almost to the point of breaking. Not fast, but super slow. One here, then wait, then another, then wait. Just like the steps I heard walking up. Like they were sneaking, and I thought, "Oh my God. There's something on the deck." I thought it had to be a big bear. So I looked, and I didn't see anything, and I looked again and saw there was a big shadow sitting in the corner. It was big. Five feet tall. Three feet wide. I asked myself if that was a bear and I got this thought, "Yes! Yes! Bear."

As soon as I got that thought, I started to be able to see the hair. And I can see through the shadow, and it looks like there's little particles, or dots, floating around in this hair. I could see the middle of it, and it looked like this long, shiny brown, beautiful hair in the middle of this indistinct ball. I said out loud, "Beautiful," and the thought came to me immediately in my mind, "Beautiful. Beautiful bear." A few seconds later, the whole thing came into focus. I was looking at the back of a big, round Sasquatch. She had her arms tucked in and her head down. It looked like a big, round, hairy stump. The words are coming into my mind now quickly, saying, "Beautiful. Beautiful bear.

Then I heard the wood of my deck creak again and remembered that there were two of them. I could feel the wood of the deck creaking, and I pressed my face against the window, and I looked to the side as much as I could, and I could see his leg. A great big, black, hairy leg. It was incredibly large and muscular and covered in what looked like long, black, curly hair, like pubic hair. Curly, wiry hair. And I pulled my head back from the window and thought "No way!' The hairball just stayed there. It didn't move. And I looked again, and the leg was moving. It stepped out from the side and let me see him. It stood up tall and I looked right at him. The size of him was impossible. Nothing is ten feet tall and four feet wide. It was just crazy.

I could see the skin on his chest. Everything else except for his face was covered with hair. His face looked very much like an ancient human's. He was standing there looking down at the window and at first, he was nonchalant. Like, "Don't mind me. I'm the neighbor." When it stood up, I felt a little bit of fear, but he was outside, and I was inside. He had black eyes, and he stood there and let me know that he was the boss. He didn't have to do that, let me tell you. But he did. He leaned down and looked in the window at me and I kind of lost it a little. I'm looking at his head, and it must

be two feet wide. I leaned back again, and he made a frowning look, and I knew that he didn't like that, but his eyes lit up. His eyes rolled up into his head, and under the whites of his eyes I could see a line of light. It just lit up like a twenty-watt light bulb. It was like something from a science fiction movie. Then I was terrified. When he did that, I could feel it, and there was like this little spark that lit up in front of his face or eyes, and that was it. I got hit with a bolt of energy or something. I couldn't see it, but I sure felt it. When it hit me, I don't know if it picked me up or not, but I just fluttered like a flag in the wind. It wasn't painful, but it was bone-rattling. I could just feel my internal organs vibrating. I just folded up and fell back onto the bed, paralyzed. I couldn't move my legs. My arms just went limp. I was terrified. I've never felt that level of fear before or since. So strong. My head went down into the blankets, and I went straight to God right then. And I'm not really a religious person. I just kept saying, "God help me. God, help me." And then everything went deathly quiet.

I don't know how long I was down there. I laid there, and I was done looking out that damned window. But they weren't done. I was laying there petrified and then I started hearing the voices again. I could hear the little one, with the strange-sounding voice saying, "Move! Move! Get up!" She then went on to say, "That was Little One. That was Little One. He like you, he like you. Get up. He like you!" I looked up, and she had moved right in front of the window, and all I can see is this big, round ball of brown hair. Then I thought, "Oh my God. Where's the other one?" I could hear a rubbing sound on the logs of the side of the cabin and I knew he was still there.

Just as I was thinking that, I felt like someone touched me on my forehead. This is so crazy, but it felt just like he'd put his hand through the wall, which was impossible, and poked me right on the forehead. I don't know what to say about that. But that's what it felt like. When he did that, I just lost it. I jumped off the bed and stood there holding the covers and looking at the window and see the little one waddling slowly towards the edge of the deck. She's leaving, and it's quiet outside now. I hoped that the big one had left too, so I went over to the window and looked out. The big one was leaving the deck as well, and he looked right back at me. And then he did the craziest thing. He put his head down, put his arms over his head like he was going to dive into the water or something, and sort of slumped forward so all I could see was a bunch of black hair. And then slowly and really smoothly, he just rolled off the edge of the deck and out of sight. It looked like he just slid on his hair or something, right over the side. It didn't even look like an animal. It looked like a black blanket pulled over the side. He was just so smooth and so clever. So, so clever. None of it makes sense, but I was looking right at him.

I watched the little one waddle over to the tree line

like a bear and hunker down. She stayed there a long time. I was thinking, "What are you?" Obviously not a bear. Suddenly, she put one leg out and then popped up into a standing position. Almost like she did this incredibly fast push-up. And she popped up into the air into a standing position. One second, she was lying on the ground, and the next she was in a standing position, letting me see her completely. I was absolutely blown away. She was very clean and kept, just a beautiful creature. She was seven and a half feet tall, and I knew this was a once-in-a-lifetime thing. I lost all my fear when I saw her and just stood there in awe, but in the back of my mind I'm thinking, "Where's the big guy?" So I look up and over to the other side, and the trees that I had pruned along the side of the cabin, one of them is way too big. It's really wide. I was looking at it and knew that he was standing there. He was even duplicating branches hanging down, and I knew that there were no branches on that tree.

As soon as I saw it, he stepped out again so I could see him. He made a HUMPH sound and walks over toward the other one. He stopped twenty feet away from her, and he took this really strange posture. He kind of squatted down a little and put his arms out in front of him with his hands hanging down, like he was meditating or something, and he just froze in place. He stood there for the longest time completely still, frozen in that position. His eyes were big and round and not moving. After a long time, the little one brought her knee way up to her ear, like some kind of dance move, then she spun, put her leg down and lifted the other one. She was dancing away. She looked at me then, the only time she looked at me. Then she bent down and did this, like, a curtsey, and then walked away into the woods.

The big guy was still there standing in position. It took a couple of steps and looked right at me in the window. He had a look in his face like he was thinking about killing me. No love in his face. We had, like, this staring contest then for a minute, and it was very uncomfortable. Like he was digging around inside me, looking inside me. It felt very creepy. He took another step, and he moved so quickly. He moved twenty or thirty feet just like that. He looked like he glided over there. He didn't walk but glided. It caught me totally off guard, and I gasped and thought, "How in the world did he do that?" He looked over at me, almost like he was amused. And then, like he wanted me to know how he moved like that, he walked back to where he started—and he did it again! It was like he understood what I was thinking. He did it again, only a bit shorter this time. It's so weird. It looked like his legs were in a blur. The top of his legs didn't move. He showed me what he was doing. Then he took a couple more steps, then looked over at me and gave me this really mean look. I don't know why. Maybe he didn't like what he saw. He took another step, and he's only got about one more step and he'll be gone. He gave me a thought then. I heard it in my mind. It said, "This didn't happen," and

I thought, "Yeah. Right. Good luck with that one." Then
he cupped both hands together, raised them, then looked
into the forest and he gave me another thought. "Forest
People. Us. Not you. This is not man. NOT man." That
just floored me and so I said to him, "You're right. This
didn't happen." But it did happen.

All these memories are burned inside my head and
they're not going anywhere. It took me years to come to
grips with what I saw. So then, the big one leaves, and
I can hear his footsteps literally shaking the ground as
he went. I breathed a sigh of relief then and thought,
'Okay. It's over. It's over.' Just as I thought that, there
came a tremendous bang on the side of the cabin. He
didn't leave, he wasn't gone at all. He was standing right
there. He had fooled me. My heart leapt into my throat,
and I'm thinking, "Is he going to come in?" So I get the
idea to run to the opposite side of the cabin, to the back
door, but I never made it. I got about halfway across the
cabin and I heard this crazy sound that sounded like an
Australian didgeridoo—those things they swing around
real fast, and they vibrate to make the sound. And I got
this vision of him making this loud, fuzzy infrasound
with his lips. His lips were vibrating. And that was it for
me. I went out. I was done. I passed out so hard and so
fast that I didn't even have time to put my hands up or
nothing.

I don't even think I was breathing. I think my heart
was flatlined. And as I was laying there on the floor, I

had an out-of-body experience. I could literally see myself lying there, and I'm up above it looking down at it. I thought, "Well, shit, I've got to get back down there." And I tried and tried to get back to my body, but it wasn't happening. I couldn't get back down there. Then I heard that voice again. The last thing it said to me was, "Stop," and I thought, "Stop what?' I didn't know what was going on. And then when it said stop, suddenly it all stopped, and I could breathe again. My heart started beating again, pounding in my chest. In the distance, I could hear what sounded like somebody gagging like they were coming up out of the water gasping for air. Trying to catch their breath. And then I realized that it's me making that noise. I wasn't breathing. I was dead.

When I came to, I remembered absolutely everything. That hadn't changed at all, but my tongue was bit, my wrist was bit. My knee was sore. I was banged up pretty good from falling on the floor that hard. I just crawled over to the bed and lay down. I knew what had happened. But I didn't want to believe any of it, of course. It was much easier to believe it was all a dream, but it was all too real. The next day, it was around noon before I could muster up enough courage to go outside. I couldn't just lay there forever. I knew I would have to get up eventually. I opened the door and looked out. All the floorboards on the deck were bent and cracked. They were tongue in groove boards and some of them were mashed up out of position. So that was it. I was hoping against hope that it *was* all a bad dream but, after seeing this, the reality of what happened to me was confirmed. So I went back inside and had another couple cups of coffee. Eventually I did go outside and found footprints and measured the approximate height of the little one against the branches where she was standing. Measured how tall the big one was. Saw the prints. One interesting thing about the prints: the ground was hard, but the grass was all mashed down where they walked.

It all happened in that one night. I never saw them again. I had to stay one more night, as I had nowhere to go. That next morning I left. I had to come back to the cabin one more time to get some stuff. After two weeks I went back. I was just going to be there long enough to grab my stuff and leave. I decided to walk around the cabin one more time and I saw where the big guy had sat down and leaned back and pushed back the logs that I had piled there for firewood. He left an indention in the woodpile. It was like he was saying, "You're gone now and I'm still here. Who owns the cabin now?"

A couple of years later, my mother wanted to go up there, so I took her. There were three of us. Me and my girlfriend and my mom. And my girlfriend and I went out for a little while. Mom stayed there in the house, and when we came back, the doors were locked. And I banged and banged on the door yelling, "Mom! Mom! What's wrong? Answer the door." And there was no response. So I think that I'm going to have to break in the door, that something had happened to her, and my girlfriend yells for her, "Mom! Mom!" in her voice, and then the door opens a little bit and Mom peeks out. I pushed the door open, and there she is sitting in a chair right beside the door holding a machete. And she was terrified, white as a ghost. And I said, "What the hell? What happened? What's wrong? Why didn't you open the door when I yelled?" And she looks at me and says, "What the hell did you do? What the hell did you do here?" I looked at her and I'm just speechless. And I said, "What are you talking about? What happened?" And all she said was, 'I thought it was you. I thought it was you.' And I said, 'You thought what was me?' And all she would say was, "Oh, Jesus Christ!" I couldn't get her to say anything else about it. That's all I could get out of her.

She wouldn't say what happened to her, but knowing what good imitators they are, I can make a pretty good guess. More than a guess: Big guy sees us coming in. Momma got left alone. He went over and knocked on the cabin. She heard my voice, thought it was me, looked out and saw him. That would be my guess. One more thing: when we were up there the last time, the woodpile was still there just like I, or he, left it, but he had pushed out two logs and stood them up where he knew I would see them. It was like he was waving goodbye to me.

Nobody ever went to that cabin after that, which was a real shame. The cabin had been in our family for years, and we just abandoned it because of those things. So those were the things that I saw. Those were the things that really happened. You know, dreams don't leave footprints and bent deck boards. I left there a different person, and it took me a long time to accept what happened, but everything I told you is true.

Those pesky Giganto Apes sure do have some funny ways about them, don't they? Folks, in this book I've tried to reiterate with each passing story that these creatures are not of this world. If they are purely flesh and blood creatures, which is the least likely origin of these things, they must be from the underground, living in cave systems and subterranean caverns deep beneath the earth. That's the only possible explanation, in my opinion. I hesitate to call them a species of anything. They would be more aptly described as "entities." Or, as Barton Nunnelly calls them, Inhumanoids. And, speaking of underground cave systems, our final stop on this journey is in Kentucky, the Bluegrass State. Home of the largest natural underground cavern system in the known world: Mammoth Caves.

8

My Old Kentucky Hell
– Barton's Story

I mentioned Barton Nunnelly in the beginning of this book and how his amazing book, *The Inhumanoids: Real Encounters with Beings That Can't Exist* inspired me to do what I do today. In fact, if it weren't for this one book, it's likely that no one would have ever even known my name. I've read thousands of books, hundreds on this and other Fortean subjects, and I, and thousands of others, consider Barton to be one of the greatest Fortean writers of all time, and his *Inhumanoids* the best book that has ever been written on the subject, surpassing Keel and Vallée and all the prominent Bigfoot researchers both past and present. Barton is so humble that, after many tries, I finally reached out to him to buy some books to give away on my podcast, only to find that he was the only author in America, and likely the world, who didn't even care to own a single copy of any of the four books that he'd penned on this subject. I know and am good friends with nearly every Fortean author on the planet, and no one is quite like Barton. He's not just an author, but a seasoned, Fortean researcher for over forty years and, unlike most other authors in the field today, Barton has seen firsthand, with his own eyes, many of the bizarre subjects he's written about. After speaking about him so much on my podcast and enlisting his help to compile the data in this book, it would be remiss of me not to speak a little about his experiences and how they seemed to all connect to that first Bigfoot looking in the window.

As has become the routine by now, it all started for him and his family back in 1971 when a Bigfoot looked into his family's kitchen window one night and scared his older sister half to death. They were living in Reed, Kentucky at the time, in Henderson County. She said the monster looked like Frankenstein, presumably because of the heavy brow ridge. His dad, Red Nunnelly, who suffered from glaucoma, had Barton's mom lead him quickly out the front door holding his .12-gauge shotgun where she saw a "brown man" running down a dirt road that led into the wooded Green River bottoms. After blasting off a few shots in the brown man's direction, everyone thought it was over.

But it was only just the beginning.

A few weeks later, as his mother, Rose, and older sister were sitting up late looking through a Sears catalogue picking out Christmas presents, they noticed a red light shining through the bedroom curtains. When Rose went to look, she saw a disc-shaped, domed object glowing red as it descended from the sky and landed behind one of the old barns on the property. Barton's family evacuated the lonely farmhouse immediately and never returned.

They moved to the city and lived there for four years, but city life wasn't for them so, in 1975 they once again moved to a small country house located in the Green River Bottoms of Spottsville, also Henderson County. Everything was fine at first until Red's chickens started disappearing. Then, Rose saw an eight-foot-tall "animal" standing on its hind legs beneath an outside light. It had red eyes and was covered with dark hair. What followed was basically an eleven-month siege of terror by multiple hairy Inhumanoids that ended up with all their farm animals dead and mutilated and the entire family fleeing the country once again.

Red and Rose had been warned from the beginning that the previous resident had seen a tall, hairy "fellow" standing at the back screen door. The previous resident had fired multiple shots through the door, but the fellow had run off, apparently unharmed. The patriarch of the family didn't think it was anything that a shotgun couldn't take care of. But he was wrong.

Not long after, a lone hunter came wandering up from one of the lower fields next to the river. He told

Red and Rose that he'd just been hunting down the river a little way and had scared up a large, hairy animal that ran on two legs. He didn't know what kind of animal it was, even though he'd spent the last ten years as a big game hunter and guide out west, but whatever it was, it was heading this way and, having heard that a family with six children had recently moved into the old Hughes farmhouse, thought he should warn us. He'd walked a good distance out of his way to do that. They became friends almost immediately. It was a friendship that would prove invaluable to the family later on. All but one, the baby, of the six Nunnelly children ended up seeing the creatures. One of them, Barton's older brother, Dean, saw it plainly in broad daylight and said it was about ten feet tall, covered in red hair that was silvery tipped, as if it were quite old. Some of the hair was thinner in the chest area, and he could see that its skin was white beneath the hair. It had black eyes, a flat nose, and a squared jaw.

Many other people saw the things as well, including friends of the family, both skeptics and believers as well. Everyone that knew Red knew that he was a straight shooter and not prone to telling lies or tall tales. He was an extremely tough and uncommonly intelligent man, having formerly been a Union County Deputy Sheriff and a Golden Glove boxing champion back in his Army days, among many other things. He'd never lost a fight in his life, even during the years he worked as a bouncer in the rough and tumble Southside bars up in Chicago.

Red Nunnelly could outthink or outfight his way out of any situation—except this one.

He was at a loss to understand what these things were that were plaguing his family. None of them had ever heard of Bigfoot. The creatures became bolder, walking around outside at night, banging on walls and screaming. It even walked up onto the porch one night and let out a low growl that rumbled through the chests of everyone in the house. Now, in addition to their own animals that died at the hands of the giant monsters, they were leaving the carcasses of animals they killed on neighboring farms right outside the Nunnelly house. No scavenger would eat the dead animals, which were all mutilated the same way; sliced down the middle with all soft tissue, including the eyes and tongues, removed. Not even a fly would land on the carcasses, and so their bodies lay on the property for months before finally decomposing. Red expressly forbade anyone to touch the dead animals or even go near them.

After months of terror and not knowing what else to do, Red finally broke down and started calling the State Police to come out and see what the hell this "intruder" was. They would come out with lights flashing and the creatures would simply melt back into the woods. Then, after they would find nothing and leave the area, out the creatures would come to start their frightful game anew. After several calls to the police in the coming weeks, Red would use the presence of the officers as an escort to load the family up and drive everyone into town to stay with his mother until things "calmed down." But they never did.

The Nunnellys weren't the only ones seeing the "Spottsville Monster" as it was dubbed by the local newspaper. Reports were coming in from all over the areas of Spottsville, Reed, and Bluff City. Red's new friend had been busy with the creatures as well. They had kept in touch by telephone since they met, as his friend only lived a mile down the road, and, when things ramped up and Red expressed concern for his safety, he had promised to come and try to track down this thing. He was sympathetic to Barton's dad, as he suffered from advanced-stage glaucoma in both eyes, and his sight was extremely limited. He couldn't track the creatures, he soon discovered, as they left no tracks, even in freshly plowed soil, but he did see the things several times, much to his regret. Once, as he stepped up into an open-ended barn to get out of the rain, he turned around, only to find himself staring into the lower chest of one of the monsters. He stood six feet, three inches tall but had to look straight up to look into the monster's eyes.

He wished he hadn't done that immediately, because the thing's eyes were blood red, and as he reached for his rifle slung across his shoulder, he became paralyzed. Then the creature spoke telepathically to him, saying, "Don't be afraid. I won't hurt you." The thing turned and ran out the other end of the barn into a muddy field—and left no footprints.

Another time, he had come upon an old, long-abandoned house in the woods while out searching and saw the creature staring at him out a window from the inside of the house. He raised his rifle and set his sight directly center on the thing's face but, before he could pull the trigger, it vanished right before his eyes. Thirty years later, when Barton interviewed him, he was surprised to learn that the creatures this man saw were different than the ones his family had seen. Whereas the ones Barton's family had witnessed looked like a "typical" Bigfoot, the ones this man had seen had long hair (like a hippie's), long, razor-sharp claws, and pointed fangs. According to him, he had seen this creature or another one like it stepping out of what he called "portals" on three different occasions. This was all a bit much for any man to take, and he was starting to wonder what he'd gotten himself into, but he persevered on for the sake of the Nunnelly children. Meanwhile, Red was trying everything he could to rid the family of these giant monsters. One night he invited five or six people to climb up to their rooftop, heavily armed, and wait for the creature to show up, then kill it. It showed up and everyone opened fire, but no monster was killed. The next day another mutilated dog carcass was lying in the spot where the monster had stood.

By now, the police had flat out refused to answer any more of the Nunnelly calls for help, and it fell to Red's friend, who was the only other person he could call within driving distance, to come escort the family away from the property when things got bad, always late in the night.

Other things happened there as well, apart from the Inhumanoid activity. The area had long been, and still is, known as a hotspot for UFO sightings. One night, a terrific thunderstorm deposited thousands of tropical fish on the Nunnelly farm. Barton claims to have seen a cloud bank open one day while returning from a trip to town. "It opened up into this perfectly round circle, and inside the circle, I could see an old-style castle with ramparts, spires, and pennants streaming in the wind. It was so clear that I could have counted the stones in the walls," he told me.

Barton was later able to trace the history of that house as far back as 1935, with every single resident he was able to speak to claiming that they were run out of the place by unknown creatures. This happened to the Nunnelly family as well, in the end, although his parents struggled hard to keep it. Things got so bad there at the end that his mother and father had decided on a plan to burn the house down with everyone inside rather than facing the prospect of the monster crashing through the door and making off with one of their children. That was the best plan they could come up with under these circumstances. Best to all just go to heaven together rather than face a lifetime knowing that one of their kids was taken in such a manner.

It all ended when Red's friend, suffering greatly

from the stress associated with the presence of these things, checked himself in to the psych ward at a local hospital where he spent two weeks. After he got home, he told Red that these things were supernatural, and they couldn't be killed or interfered with. If one of them decides to take one or all of the kids, there would be nothing anyone could do. You would just never see the kids again.

The next day they all packed their belongings and moved back to the city. Rose and Red's marriage lasted only three months after their departure and the family split up, never to be the same again. Barton blames it on the monster, and who could blame him? Red's helpful friend suffered a heart attack soon afterward, during which he had an out-of-body experience. The doctors saved his life and he awakened with psychic powers. He could see auras around people and could communicate with, or rather influence the actions of, animals such as deer and dogs. Both he and his wife have seen the creatures on multiple occasions as recently as 2019.

Whatever the Spottsville Monster was and is, it's still there.

Conclusion

Folks, I've given you several cases here which I hope you come away from with a new understanding of Bigfoot phenomena, *all* the phenomena associated with Bigfoot. It's my opinion that if there is such a thing as a strictly flesh and blood Bigfoot, they must live deep underground hidden away from all prying eyes and are only seen when they want to be. Kentucky, it would seem, would be an ideal place for these physical creatures as it contains the largest underground cavern system in the known world, Mammoth Cave, located in central Kentucky. Nearly all the cases examined in this book seem to be in direct opposition to that theory and, in my opinion, the ape, or flesh and blood theory is the least likely of all to be the correct one, even though the main body of all Bigfoot reports are made up of run-of-the-mill, mundane encounters or sightings. However, atypical Bigfoot reports, along with a seemingly ongoing and long-standing relationship with other anomalous entities are becoming increasingly more common. Or maybe they've always been this common and the witnesses were simply too afraid to tell the whole story. As I said at the beginning of this work, I've interviewed hundreds of people regarding the Bigfoot subject, and I have scores more reports just like these, that just don't fit into the neatly constructed box that science has manufactured. Ignoring reports such as these only proves to further darken the murky waters that this subject is submerged beneath. We need to shed some new light on those waters, looking beyond the surface of what we are meant to see, to what we *need* to see to understand the truth. Light that goes wherever the evidence leads it, and not just to where the researcher allows it to. It's time for a new understanding of these creatures to take hold. A truer understanding. I hope that this book has helped at least one person to take that first step toward understanding the Bigfoot phenomena.

THE END

Biography

Josh Turner was born and raised in Texas. Ever since he was a child, he has been aware of the paranormal through his own experiences. His love for the paranormal led to him to collecting stories and eventually podcasting. Possibly the single most important encounter with the paranormal was in his hometown in Texas in 1990, when he and his best friend encountered an upright canid creature. Ever since then Josh has been on a quest for answers. He has spent his life interviewing hundreds of people regarding the paranormal, cryptids, and unexplained. Josh enjoys hosting his podcast, *Paranormal Round Table,* where he talks about all things paranormal with his cohosts. On this podcast he has interviewed many authors, field researchers, and a multitude of experiencers.

Paranormal Round Table can be found on
YouTube Livestream every Friday and Sunday,
and podcast episode on Tuesdays found on YouTube,
Spotify and all major podcast platforms.